Ride the Wave
Journey from the Inside Out

Aviva Barnett, LSW

MWmindworks, LLC
3 Forest Ct.
Passaic, NJ 07055
mwmindworks.com

Printed in the United States of America
First Edition

ISBN-13: 978-1514774892
ISBN-10: 1514774895

Typesetting and Cover Design by: Devorah Jacobowitz
Editing by: Alisa Roberts

I dedicate this book to
my clients.
I am honored to be a part of
your transformative journey.
Your courage motivates me,
your faith inspires me and
your innocence touches me.

יחיאל מיכל טווערסקי

כ״ק אַדמו״ר הרה״צ כמוהר״ר יעקב ישראל זצלה״ה מהאָרנאָסטי־פאָל

Rabbi Michel Twerski

ב״ה

Cheshvon 20, 5776

I have had occasion to peruse sections of Aviva Barnett's book, <u>Ride the Wave</u>, and have been impressed with the quality and integrity of her work. The Innate Health philosophy, which is largely the backdrop of Mrs. Barnett's manuscript, is based upon a straightforward, common sense understanding of how human beings engage and respond to the ongoing challenges of life, great and small. The counsel of <u>Ride the Wave</u> is transformative, and quickly grasped by an open mind. While there are an increasing number of books and articles published in recent years which draw upon this approach, Mrs. Barnett's work engages the reader on a more spiritual plane, clearly drawn from Mrs. Barnett's own exciting journey, which makes it all the more real. I believe that everyone will easily identify with this presentation, and will benefit significantly by adopting the compelling ideas which grow organically from the premises she describes.

I sincerely hope this work will be received warmly by the many who seek to build a healthier self, and offer my humble blessings for continued success.

Sincerely

Rabbi Michel Twerski

Congregation Beth Jehudah • 3100 N. 52nd Street • Milwaukee, WI 53216 • ph. 414 442-5730 • Fax 414 442-6171
Home Study • 3259 N. 51st Boulevard • Milwaukee, WI 53216 • ph. 414 442-6983 • Fax 414 447-6995

Acknowledgments

Aleeza Ben Shalom, the visionary and motivator behind this project—your support, focused dedication and belief in me and my message gave me the courage to begin this journey. Thank you for being my cheerleader.

Alisa Roberts, my editor, thank you for your endless patience. Your creativity never ceased to amaze me. Your tweaks always managed to take what I wrote and make it better. Most of all, I appreciate your determination to keep "my voice" throughout the process.

Devorah Jacobowitz, my graphic designer and friend, your talent has no end. From the logo, book cover and formatting, to my boys' bar mitzvah monograms, you're the best. Your attention to detail and drive for perfection is what made this book what it is. Your generosity and caring inspires me.

Erika Bugbee, Brian and Terry Rubenstein, Yanky Raskin and **Rebecca London**, thank you for taking the time to read the manuscript and for your valuable input.

Leah Damski, thank you for your creativity with the titles. It pulled the theme of the book together.

A special friend, for teaching and training me with all of your heart. I owe the person I am today and where I am professionally to you. Although we have taken different paths,

I have unending gratitude for all you gave me—your time, your depth of understanding, your patience and your belief in me.

Simi Yellen and **Melissa Stein**, what a gift to have true friends like you. I am grateful for your support, coaching and guidance. We make a great team.

Lisa Schwartz, Mitch and Karen Kuflik, thank you for your friendship and encouragement. I appreciate your backing this project.

Rav Michel and Rebbetzen Twerski, the Twerski Wellness Institute team and all my colleagues, thank you for your endorsement and for allowing me to be part of the vision to help the Jewish people via the Principles of Innate Health.

My in-laws, thank you for the gift of your son, your love and always showering me with compliments.

My parents, thank you for the endless help you have given me and my family in every aspect of our lives. We feel your love in all you do.

My children, **Aryeh, Dovid, Shmuli** and **Akiva**, you are precious to me, and I love you dearly. May each one of you find your own unique light and shine it into the world.

Simcha, my husband, my partner and my hero. Thank you for your unending love and support. I truly felt it throughout this whole process. Your edits were invaluable. I am grateful that we are on this journey together.

The One Above, thank You for my blessed life, my journey and the gift to be able to guide others in revealing their innate health and bringing them closer to You.

Table of Contents

Preface

When I was young, we used to go to the beach. We would always try to ride the waves. You have to be in just the right spot at just the right time and then...Jump! Swim! Stroke! And *ride the wave*! When you hit it right, it was so much fun riding the wave all the way to the shore.

Of course, there were times where it appeared to me as if I wasn't in the right spot at the right time. I would miss the wave, or the wave would be too small to carry me. Then I would have to wait for the next one, or if I tried for the wave anyway, it would crash over me really hard. One wave I tried to catch crashed over me so hard it dragged me under. I was pushed and pulled, sand flying in the water, salt water up my nose, until the power of the wave subsided and I could get up and get my bearings.

It felt so bad, but once I got over it, I was back in the water, waiting for another wave to ride. Lucky for me, there was always another wave coming. I never had to get too upset or wait too long for another wave. Maybe it wasn't a very windy day so the waves were small; maybe it was a crazy windy day and the waves were gigantic. Either way, the security I felt knowing that another wave was always coming gave me hope and the freedom to keep at it.

Regardless of the type of wave that came, it was never about me. I didn't create the waves, I couldn't control the waves and it wasn't my fault if they were too big or too small. There was never anything personal to feel about the way the waves came or broke on the shore. All I did was show up and ride the wave that came. Some were more fun than others, some were a bit painful, but I could always ride what was in front of me and bank on the fact that another one was coming soon.

Our thinking is like the waves in the ocean. There is always another thought coming. If I could "ride the wave" of my thinking—that is, relate to my thinking like the waves in the ocean (i.e., that there is nothing personal about them)—I'd navigate life with grace more of the time. I'd be psychologically free. Just as I don't create, can't control and don't take blame for the waves in the ocean, I don't create thought, can't control thought and am not to blame for the thoughts in my mind. This freedom allows me to show up today and ride the next wave of thought that comes.

Many of us crave emotional well-being, yet we find it elusive and wonder why. Could we be emotionally healthy regardless of what or who is around us? Do we have within us the clarity and wisdom we need to navigate the terrain God has placed before us? Can we access insight that could transform our lives? Imagine if we weren't limited by the spinning, crazy, never-ending chatter in our mind and we could tap into the abundance of mental health that we already possess (even if we don't know it yet).

What would life be like if we weren't victims to our own thinking? What if we weren't afraid of making mistakes; concerned with what others think of us; worried about what our kids are or aren't doing; anxious about money, our jobs or the fridge breaking; insecure about whether our parents approve of our choices, or if our husbands love us, or whether we will ever get married?

The goal of this book is to share with you an understanding of how human beings function psychologically. In the wake of hope and freedom, you will be able to navigate life's ups and downs with a sense of inner peace and connection. Like every author, I have my own style. I am sharing my journey of awakening to this understanding through the context of my personal life. I share my own personal struggles as well as those of my clients in order to provide a space for you to learn something that has been invaluable in my life.

I am an observant Jewish mother of four sons,

each of whom is highly active, independent and spirited in his own way. I am a dedicated and supportive wife, counselor and life coach, as well as an adult educator on Jewish subject matters. For me personally, an important aspect in learning about this understanding is that it is consistent with the Jewish wisdom by which I live my life.

Some of the examples and analogies given in this book are in the context of my religious affiliation. That may or may not be your cup of tea, but I invite you to read beyond the manner in which I choose to share my experience and remain focused on the deeper message that is at play throughout this book.

In teaching, I have witnessed the following miracles that are available for all human beings, regardless of religious affiliation:

☞ Freedom from a life of eating disorders and addictions.

☞ Inner peace and joy after years of anxiety and depression.

☞ Rediscovery of love in marriages on the brink of divorce.

☞ Inner wisdom and patience guiding parents who had been at their wits' end.

☞ Intimacy and closeness in a relationship where lack of connection was the norm.

☞ Inner confidence, flexibility and presence to life instead of everyday annoyances, frustrations and stresses.

☞ Flexibility, being able to take life in stride, even when thrown a curveball.

- Acceptance and understanding replacing anger and upset around life's circumstances.
- Compassion and forgiveness replacing a life filled with resentment and revenge.
- A sense of trust and security that we are being guided by the Creator replacing hopelessness and fear.

INTRODUCTION

Setting Sail

MY PERSONAL STORY

TURNING OF THE TIDES

In 2006, I came across a whole new field of psychology that transformed my life. As a licensed social worker and trained life coach, I used an array of my personal experiences and professional trainings to create my own life coaching practice. I was successful at sharing tools and techniques which enabled people to eliminate their negative charge toward others, think better and reframe the way they were looking at their lives so they could feel happier.

I held people accountable; I helped them stay on track and live with integrity. There were many lists of things to do. Try this, do that, chart this, control that. To be honest, I think my clients were pretty happy with our work together and enjoyed the advice, perspective and direction I gave them.

Little did I know that I was working within a system that limited their results. In the hope of helping people in mental distress, our society has become obsessed with diagnosing every little behavior that doesn't fit into the category of "normal." With all of our advances, somehow the focus on *health* in the mental health field has been lost. With all good intentions, the mental health field tends to focus on the diagnosis of mental illness rather than on the mental well-being that exists within every human being. We will talk more about this in Chapter 2.

I came across a psychological model used by Innate Health practitioners called the Three Principles of Mind, Consciousness and Thought. It was totally different from anything I had heard before. It points to an impersonal and universal truth that all experience is generated from within via these principles. Grasping this truth for myself was a game changer that resulted in experiencing my innate well-being more often.

Following that first exposure, whenever I was working with my clients, I insightfully noticed that if they were to understand the role of thought and consciousness, I wouldn't have to give them a tool or teach them a skill to relieve their upsets. There was no technique to teach about the Principles because the Principles are not something to do. Rather, they help us realize a truth about where our experience is coming from. I wanted to be able to show my clients that their feelings were coming from their thoughts in the moment; that the actual situations they were upset about were not what were creating their feelings of upset in the moment. Their upset was actually coming from their thinking about what they were upset about.

For example, Alison's [1] daughter was not married yet. Alison believed that this fact stressed her out and kept her up at night worrying. I wanted her to be able to recognize that her level of anxiety and fear about her daughter's marriage status fluctuated. Sometimes Alison felt clearly that there was a reason her daughter wasn't married yet and trusted that the extra time would be good for her daughter as she finished her degree. Other times, Alison worried about what would become of her daughter if she never married.

I knew that as her thinking shifted, so would her feeling state. I knew this to be true for myself, but I didn't know how to help Alison see that. I began to feel that I was doing my clients a disservice because I didn't have the words to share with them what I had observed for myself. I was living in the misunderstanding of where my feelings were coming from, and that misunderstanding was innocently tripping me up.

---

[1] All client names and some identifying details have been changed to protect their privacy.

It was at that point that I closed my private coaching practice to train and gain a professional level of understanding so that I could be of service to my clients on a deeper level. This was not another tool or technique I could add to my repertoire. It was a way of perceiving life and human nature. There were no how-tos, which was very different from what I had been teaching before. It was a total reorientation to the question, "Where does my experience of life come from?"

MUDDY WATERS

Before my exposure to this unique understanding, the glasses I wore, which I think 97% of the world also wears (although I made up that statistic), gave me the impression that life was coming from an external source: the world, my difficult circumstances, you. I assumed I was a victim to life and life's circumstances. I believed that I was unhappy, unsatisfied and stuck in life because of my "mommy" status.

I had big plans, big dreams. I wanted to be great, but I had these four little impediments (sorry, guys) under the age of seven in my way. The classes I took and the philosophy I heard about how my children were not in the way of my greatness but instead were my keys to greatness rarely moved me. I wanted to grow and be better, but I kept falling on my face because I found myself angry, yelling, bored, unproductive, overwhelmed and bothered all of the time. If it wasn't my kids holding me back, there were ten other things I could point to that were holding me back. There was always something to blame for my unhappiness and it rarely had anything to do with me.

If I wasn't feeling connected to my husband, I thought it was his fault. If I was angry at my kids for being wild, I thought it was their fault. If I was bothered because I had to do the laundry when none of my friends did their own laundry, I blamed it on lack of income. If I was aggravated by traffic, I blamed it on the fact that we lived out of town. I usually saw the glass as half empty, and some would have described me as a naysayer or pessimist. I believed, though, that my thinking and perspective were realistic, and sometimes even responsible, reactions to life. I believed that every thought I had was true. Really, I was an optimist wannabe. I had no idea that seeing the glass as half empty was a reflection of my unhappy feeling state, rather than an accurate representation of my life.

I didn't purposely focus on the negative. It was just a bad habit, like biting your nails or smoking. Only I didn't recognize it as a habit. I thought it was part of my nature. (Which really is code for "Please ignore it because I can't change it.") Unfortunately, I had inadvertently habituated myself to look at what was wrong, thereby focusing all my energy on the negative thoughts in my mind. So even when the family had a good day, all I noticed was the crying, whining and fighting—as if the joy, getting along and *nachas* (sweet pride) never happened.

No matter how much I tried to be grateful by writing

gratitude journals or listing all the things I loved about my husband, my children or my life, it didn't seem to change the way I felt for more than a day or two. No matter how many classes I listened to about how great it is to raise and mold children, they didn't change the way I felt for long.

When human beings have a misunderstanding about where their internal experience is coming from, they tend to look outside of themselves for relief. Relief, however, is an inside job.

In the brief moments I was relieved of my habitual thinking, I was able to appreciate that I really had a blessed life: a loving husband who listened to and supported me, healthy children who were full of life and personality, parents who would do anything for me and my children, in-laws who were easy to be around, opportunities to share the beauty of a meaningful Jewish life with all kinds of Jews, a roof over our heads...the list could go on. However, outside of those brief moments of relief, my incessant negative thoughts plagued me. The ramifications of believing these thoughts affected all of my relationships.

MAKING WAVES

As an example, I constantly thought about how my husband and I were doing as a couple and constantly evaluated how connected we were. If I was feeling distant or disconnected, it never occurred to me that the feeling came from a thought I was having. I thought my feelings came from his behavior. I believed he was making me feel disconnected.

We would spend time together and I'd feel like he wasn't emotionally available. He would tell me he was just distracted about work, but I never believed him. Instead, I would become sensitive and withdrawn; I'd be down for days and make him pay for not talking to me. I took the distance personally and thought, "He doesn't want to be close to me, therefore he must not love me." Layers of insecurity and judgment swam around in my head.

In a talk I heard by Cathy Casey, a Three Principles facilitator, she said, "You can only experience someone as difficult if you are having 'difficult' thinking about them." Meaning, I can only experience my husband as disconnected if I am having a lot of thoughts about how disconnected we are. I was creating my own sensation of disconnection and blaming it on him; unwittingly, I might add.

Layers of insecurity and judgment didn't only show up around my husband. They were with me all day, especially surrounding how I was raising my children. But since I had no visibility to these thoughts, I spent all my time blaming my children for my unhappiness and my inability to get anything done. Believing all of my judgmental thinking at times didn't bode well for my children. When you believe they are to blame, it looks like a good idea to yell at them for everything they do wrong. Take it from me, this doesn't make for a warm and cozy environment.

TESTING THE WATERS

A friend of mine had trained with Pransky and Associates, an organization dedicated to teaching the message of the Three Principles of Innate Health to both clients and practitioners. She wanted to start teaching, so I offered to be her first student. Going to her house was like going to another place and time. She gave me fresh-squeezed grapefruit juice; there was a fire burning in the fireplace; and it was quiet, like a Vermont lodge, with candles flickering. We took a seat on the couch in front of the fireplace, and I started talking. This was definitely not the traditional therapy I had been used to.

She asked me what I would like to talk about. With an opening like that, I just started spewing off a few problems. The more I talked about them, the angrier I got and the faster I spoke. After a while of me talking, she asked, "Would you mind if we put the 'problem' on the back burner for a while and talk about the nature of thought?" What choice did I have? So I said, "I guess not."

She asked, "Where do good feelings come from?"

I was stumped. She was asking me a question I had no answer to. I mean, I am the touchy-feely type; shouldn't I have thought about this before?

"Don't worry, we'll come back to that later," she said confidently. "Where does thought come from?"

"Thought?" I asked. I wondered, "Am I hearing her correctly? What does this have to do with my problems?"

"Yes." She sat patiently, like she had all the time in

the world. I, of course, was searching my brain for the right answer. So there was a silence; awkward for me, although I sensed she was totally fine with it.

Finally she saved me from my misery and said, "It comes from the place everything comes from...God."

"Duh," I thought to myself. Then I thought, "That was a trick question. But wait a minute, what does that mean exactly? Are you saying that all thought comes from God? And what does that have to do with my problem? How are we going to solve my problems if we don't talk about them? Clearly she doesn't know a thing about therapy."

"It's not an analytic understanding," she explained. "It's a soul-like understanding, something beyond the intellect. Just get yourself out of the way and let your deeper-self listen to what I am saying." "Don't work so hard," was her constant refrain. It's like listening to music. You want to listen for a feeling that will arise within you, rather than focusing on the words.

I decided to give it a try, and we met weekly for a while. I explored the nature of thought and the concept of where thought comes from in a different way. The more I tried to figure it out, the farther away I got from sensing what she was pointing me toward.

WAKING UP

I slowly became aware of all of the thinking I was having throughout the day. Trust me, a lot of it was ugly and judgmental. Now let me be honest: I didn't know I was having judgmental thinking about everyone and everything. I just thought I was thinking the truth. I had no idea that was my judgmental habit of thought in action—and that I was feeling that.

For example, I knew I wanted serenity and calm in my life, but it looked to me like my chaotic household made that an impossibility. I didn't think that was a judgmental thought; I thought it was reality. Every time I would share with my friend about my crazy household, she would just nod with an affirming, "Uh-huh," and look like she was listening, drinking up every word, with no judgment. But I felt judgment because I was so busy judging myself as I spoke.

I call this process "waking up" to your thinking or gaining "thought visibility." I became aware of so much content that ran through my head; I had never realized it before. I never noticed the actual thoughts; I just lived in a constant state of annoyance and blamed it on the people around me. I started to realize that I had thinking like this all day long about everyone: my family, the slow check-out girl, the disorganized carpool line, the late fix-it guy...you name it.

Once I began to get visibility to my thoughts, they got louder until the negativity felt unbearable. At a certain point I wanted to rip my head off my shoulders. The thoughts were coming fast and furious and I couldn't stop them. I wanted to return to my state of ignorant bliss, and wondered why I had started playing around with this thought visibility thing in the first place.

THE COAST IS CLEAR

During that phase, I had occasions where my mind settled and quieted down. In those moments, I had a few insights. I began to see that the glasses I was wearing were faulty. I began to question the direct cause and effect relationship I had made between my husband or children's behavior and my anger, unhappiness or disconnect.

I had spent so much time focused "out there"—on the people, places and things in my life that were upsetting me and keeping me stuck—that blame seemed like the only option. I really believed my circumstances were so difficult that they made me unhappy. I started to realize that thought had a role to play in my life. I started to realize that I feel my thinking in the moment all of the time.

I saw clearly that my husband did not have a problem connecting to me. I saw the "is-ness" of life; meaning there is what is...and then there is all the thinking I get interested in and what I make it mean. For example, let's say my husband came home from work feeling stressed out and went into his office right away.

That is "what is." He is in the office. Then there was all the thinking I had and what I made it mean, such as: "he doesn't care about us, he's not available, he's distant, there must be a problem with our relationship if he can't talk to me about what is going on at work." This thought process was making it about me. Really, he just didn't want to talk about work. He wanted space—not from me, just space to unwind.

I realized that all of the stories I made up in my head were just thoughts, not necessarily reality. In the past, I would have spent hours being upset and no one would have been the wiser. I realized I was doing this to myself. I am the thinker, and who said I have to keep thinking along the same track? That track is a train wreck waiting to happen. Alternately, I could look in a different direction and perhaps wait for an insight to come that would help me better deal with the situation.

I remember one of the first times I noticed I was indulging in my disconnected habit of thinking. The minute I noticed it ("thought recognition"), I had an insight: "I am thinking disconnected thoughts and that is why I feel disconnected." The second I looked away, I felt God drop a new thought in my head: "Stop." The next one was: "Move on with life."

I saw in a flash how my thoughts played a significant role in how I was experiencing my life. It was like the speed of my thoughts slowed down, opening up a space for me, so I could observe those thoughts before I acted on them. This slowing down afforded me an enhanced level of free choice in that moment. This was something I hadn't felt before.

In time, while thoughts such as "He doesn't love me," or "There must be a problem if he doesn't want to talk to me," continued to come, they didn't have the same grip upon me. I couldn't take them as seriously as I had in the past. At some point it occurred to me to stop indulging in them altogether. My relationship to these types of thoughts shifted. Not only was I not blaming my husband for my feelings of disconnection, but I wasn't feeling disconnected to him that often anymore.

This one small adjustment has completely altered our relationship. I refuse to spend time in my head beating him up, tearing him down or making up stories. I even refuse to call my friends to discuss "what happened this time," because I know that my perspective is filled with a lot of imaginary and illusory thoughts that I don't want to give life to—and I don't want my friends to validate and give life to them either. This was huge for me. Once all of that thinking diminished, it left room for me to see him as he really is: a wonderful husband who only wants to make me happy.

As a side note for those who are feeling bothered, don't get me wrong. I understand that there are situations where "what happened this time" really may be problematic. This isn't a Pollyanna approach to life. This understanding isn't pointing toward ignoring unacceptable behavior. I'm not implying that there isn't a reality (someone hurting you or doing something you don't like). I'm suggesting that my experience of any type of behavior is coming from within me. If I make the behavior mean something about myself or if I have a lot of judgmental thinking about the behavior, I will feel that in my body as insecurity. If that happens, I am less likely to access my inner wisdom in order to differentiate between what is and what I am making it mean. Perhaps more importantly, I won't create the emotional distance required to enable insight to emerge, which would actually help me productively deal with any unacceptable behavior that needs to be dealt with.

Another profound insight I had was about my children. I constantly felt like a failure as a parent, wondering, "What am I doing wrong that my children are disrespectful, don't listen and talk back?" One afternoon as I was yelling at one of my sons and he was yelling back, it hit me: I'm feeling my thinking, not his action of yelling back. My anger is coming from all this nasty thinking I am having about my son and his behavior. I got visibility to a hidden belief (thought) that I constantly had which was: "He is doing this to me on purpose." I was taking his behavior so personally.

Once I saw that thought, it seemed preposterous. The next insightful thought I got was: "No, he's not." Insightful thoughts are usually pretty simple, but I had never heard that one before. "No, he's not." It was as if a totally original idea, a new thought, dropped into my head.

It was a vertical move rather than a horizontal move. A horizontal move might be trying to convince myself it was preposterous or trying to reframe his behavior. A vertical move lifted me into a higher level of consciousness. Imagine a bird perched on a telephone wire looking down at life with more perspective. The thought just popped in my mind, without any work on my part, and shifted the whole relationship I had to his behavior. It occurred to me: Why would a child do this on purpose?

Now, I am not implying that my son was an angel. The reality was that he did do disrespectful things, as many children do. But my feelings of anger were not coming from his actions; they only magnified his actions. They were coming from the thinking I was having about his actions and what I made his actions mean. As I continued to move vertically, I could feel the weight of all my thoughts being lifted, and I ceased having feelings of anger around the same disrespectful actions. How was that possible?

SHIFTING CURRENTS

This shift is possible because we feel what is on our mind in the moment. That being the case, it is no wonder I was feeling anger, frustration and tension—as if I were going to explode—while I was thinking, "He is doing this to me on purpose!" From this feeling state, I was unable to access any wisdom about how to respond to his behavior in a productive, educational fashion. My personal overlay magnified things in a way that blocked me from accessing wisdom on what I needed to do and how to respond maturely.

When the thoughts shifted, so did the feeling. "No he's not," had a settled, peaceful quality to it. From this feeling state, I had a better chance to access wisdom that could guide me in responding to his behavior. I had more wits about me to teach him what is appropriate and OK without all the negativity and judgment. In this space, I started to catch sight of the fact that just as I get lost in my habitual thinking, so do my children.

When I talk about the feeling state, I am not speaking about an emotional state, but a physical sensation in my body. The ability to listen to my feeling state means that when I feel tension, tightness, my heart pounding (which can show up as stress, anxiety or anger), my feeling state is an indicator, a barometer, as to the quality of my thinking in the moment. So too, when I feel relaxed, light, my heart calm (which can show up as peaceful, grateful or connected), my feeling state is an indicator or barometer as to the quality of my thinking in the moment.

I became quite familiar with the intense, compelling feeling of urgency I walked around in for much of my day. From this feeling state, my relationship to time becomes skewed. Everything appears like it has to be done now; there's not a minute to waste. The intensity is so profound that it's as if my mind is frozen on what has to happen now and I feel like I'll explode if it doesn't.

Can you relate to that feeling? The feeling of I *have* to say it now, I *have* to do it now, I *have* to eat or drink now, I *have* to send that email now, I *have* to answer that phone now. I usually felt it at bedtime or when it was time to get the kids out to school. I felt it when we were late or when

I wanted something done my way. I experimented and learned to wait it out until the intensity passed through my body.

When it passed, it was a good indication that the quality of my thinking had shifted. Once a shift occurs, what feels so urgent can actually look quite silly. When I understand that my feeling state is coming from thought, it doesn't look like a good idea to blame my circumstances.

Have you ever noticed how much energy we expend in trying to control and manipulate our environment in an attempt to find happiness? This is actually a recipe for failure and frustration because it is not the circumstance that is creating our unhappiness; it is our busy mind thinking about the circumstance that is creating our unhappiness. Now, instead of exerting tons of energy trying to control the circumstances, I wait until my mind settles and I get my bearings back.

SMOOTH SAILING

Practically, once I started to sense for myself how human beings work, I began to navigate my relationship with my husband more gracefully. Like all relationships, the feelings between us can get heated. I am committed to listening to my feeling state as a guide when we talk so that, as often as humanly possible, I have warm feelings for him when we have to discuss something. I also like to wait until he has warm feelings for me.

If it's a difficult issue and we can't talk about it

calmly, I try not to talk about it. I understand clearly that nothing good will come of it if we try to talk to each other from an urgent place. I have learned this from experience time and time again, and yet I can still forget it. That means that if while we are talking I start to feel frustrated or I can sense my husband is getting annoyed, I will say (although not always as lovingly as I would like), "Can we talk about this later?" Eventually, the intensity passes and then we try again.

This can happen a few times before we are really ready to talk, and that's alright. No pressure, nothing wrong here, just give it another shot until we can talk to each other in a pleasant way. This is actually counter to the marriage advice my mother believed, which was: "Never go to bed angry." If you follow that advice, you have to talk out whatever is making you angry that day. But two angry people talking escalates into two angrier people fighting. However, if you wait it out and sleep on it, the intensity has a chance to pass and you might even wake up with a fresh perspective.

Can you grasp how practical and helpful this could be in marriage (or any relationship, for that matter)? There are many things in life that have to be dealt with, such as finances, health, raising kids, picking schools, being in or out of work, being overworked, dating, etc. My goal here is not to ignore talking about life, but to know when to talk about life. If I wait for a healthy state of mind, it will probably allow room for a constructive conversation to take place, which will be more effective.

It can really look like the circumstances of our lives are what make us stressed out, overwhelmed and unhappy. Until we discover the pivotal role thought plays in those circumstances. Now I don't get duped as often into thinking it's my circumstances that are creating my feelings. This is a game changer in how people experience their day-to-day lives.

Said another way, the circumstance is what it is: my child did what he did or said what he said and the natural consequences of that action are what they are. But as my thinking fluctuates around what is, so does the way I relate to what is, because there is never only one way to relate to any situation. Although there may be a real circumstance—my child said or did something and has the consequences to deal with—I get that my state of mind is what determines how I experience it. There is what is and then there is my overlay on what is, which is what creates my experience of it.

Sometimes I think a circumstance is a real problem, other times a challenging opportunity; sometimes it's no big deal, and other times it feels like the end of the world. None of these is right or wrong; they are each just what I am going through at the time. The internal shift of knowing my experience is coming from my thinking instead of the circumstances has been profound in every area of my life.

Although nothing externally has changed, it feels as if everything has changed. I enjoy life so much more now.

I don't take myself or my thinking so seriously. I don't take my bad moods so seriously. I don't take other people's thinking or actions so seriously because I know it is just a reflection of their state of mind rather than a reflection of me. I don't personalize everything anymore. I feel psychologically free, not trapped like an animal in a cage clawing to get out, with no free will to do so. I used to live in annoyance and irritation constantly and only visit inner peace temporarily. Now I live with a sense of inner peace and connection and visit annoyance and irritation. I am extremely grateful for this understanding in my life and hope you will benefit from it as well.

PART I

YOU CAN'T CONTROL THE WAVES, BUT YOU CAN LEARN HOW TO SURF

Understanding the Principles Behind Our Psychological Functioning

CHAPTER 1

Catch the Next Wave

HOW TO READ THIS BOOK

I want to suggest a way to read this book in order to get the most benefit. Have you ever looked at a 3D stereogram image? It's where one picture is hidden behind another and you have to stare until your eyes go cross-eyed...and then an image appears. If you can't see the image, they give you a few tips to help: allow your eyes to relax; don't just stare *at* the image, try to stare *through* it. You'll notice your eyes will go slightly out of focus. If you don't know what I mean, google 3D stereograms and try one.

If you are someone who looks at the picture and gets frustrated that you can't discover the hidden image, the frustration actually makes it harder to see. Your eyes will do the opposite of relaxing. You will start focusing more closely and trying to look harder. It's counterintuitive. At some point, for most people, your eyes relax and an image emerges.

The understanding I am speaking about is sort of like trying to discover an image behind another image. We have the illusion of life as an image and we are trying to see beyond it. Don't just stare *at* the illusion of life, try to stare *through* it. As your mind relaxes something emerges: a picture beyond what you previously were able to see.

So when you find yourself saying "*How?*" throughout this book, remember to relax. Working harder will make it harder to notice, but I give you my word: if you hang in there, the image of a hopeful, peaceful and resilient life will emerge.

A NEW WAY TO SURF

Once I was frying *latkes* (potato pancakes) for my kids and one of them asked if he could flip the potatoes. The conversation went something like this:

Me: "It's not a good idea because the pan and oil are very hot and I don't want you to get burned."

My son: "It's fine, Mom. OOUUCCHH!"

Me: "Didn't I just tell you it was hot?"

My son: "I wanted to see for myself."

There is a real difference between knowing something because someone tells you and knowing something from your own experience. There is something about having your own experience that takes the level of knowledge to a different place, beyond just being an idea.

Have you ever seen someone notice a sign that says "Wet Paint" and then touch the paint? It's as if they didn't know the paint was wet until they touched it themselves. With paint on their finger, they could say, "Yeah, this really is wet paint."

In school, we were taught many things. We were trained by our teachers or professors to take copious notes in order to memorize material and be able to regurgitate it back. Although amassing information is valuable, information in our heads alone is not the experience of the information. No one would allow a doctor to perform surgery on them without the doctor having some experience in the operating room, no matter how much book knowledge he has. There is a difference between intellectually knowing how to perform a surgery and what to do if a crisis arises, and having the experience of performing surgery and responding to a crisis.

It's the same with this type of learning. Learning to orient ourselves toward insight is not going to happen simply because we amass a lot of information about how to do it. Our intellectual abilities, though respectable, aren't able to guide us here. The goal is not for you to acquire more information from another book, but for you to find the internal wisdom and common sense that you already possess.

Real change is not an intellectual idea. It's an experience. Intellectually grasping ideas doesn't create change. Shifts that transform lives happen on a deeper level, an experiential level. What's the difference?

Imagine I want to teach my five-year-old how to ride a bike. I could give him all the instruction in the world. "These are the pedals. You have to move them really fast so you don't fall. When you find yourself leaning to one side, move your body to the other. Keep the handlebars straight unless you need to turn, and then only turn them slightly, not too quickly."

At the end of this intellectual discourse on riding a bike, will my child know how to ride a bike? Will he know what balance feels like? No, because balance is not an intellectual idea; it's an experience. Once he gets on the bike and rides and falls and rides and falls, he will gain a feeling of balance for himself. The feeling of his body leaning one way and trying to come back to center will be his own experience of finding balance. Once he has that, he will always be able to ride. But that can't be explained intellectually. A person has to get on a bike to understand balance, to feel it, to know it.

Nice ideas and good advice are not in the realm of personal experience, but rather in the realm of the intellect. Has anyone ever given you good advice? Here are some examples of good advice: "You should try this great new food plan!"; "This is how to respond to your children when they are acting out in a certain way..."; "Communicate like this during a fight with your husband." Then we go and try to implement the good advice, are disappointed by failed results and wonder, "It was such great advice. Why didn't it work? What's my problem?"

The truth is you don't have a problem. It's just that good advice only moves us if we see it for ourselves. If we have an insight, a sight from within, where we actually perceive with our mind's eye the soundness of the advice, then transformation begins. Most of the time people only listen to good advice from an intellectual perspective, and that can't transform a person. We want to learn to orient ourselves to be able to listen for that voice from within.

A shift occurs when we listen from a deeper place, from a soulful place, from an experiential place. What does it mean to listen from a deeper place? Imagine a vessel, for example, a ceramic bowl. The bigger and deeper it is, the more it can contain. Did you ever receive a package that appeared huge only to open it and find tons of tissue paper with a small present sitting on top? That's an example of wasting the vessel.

We each have this big, deep vessel—our mind—that has the potential to hold all the wisdom we need to live our lives, but we naively fill it up with lots of useless tissue paper: our unhelpful, distracted, personal thinking. If we become conscious of this fact, we make room to listen for something new. If our minds are filled up with all the thoughts we already know, then there is no room to listen for something else.

This is a different type of learning than what we are

used to, and this book will probably be a different reading experience too. It may at times seem repetitive, but that is alright because I am not trying to just share information with you. That would be a cognitive process about intellectual ideas. Instead, I want to create space for a realization from within, enabling movement to occur. Since all human beings are touched in different ways, repeating ideas from different angles provides more of an opportunity for a shift to occur for you.

KEEPING LIFE AT BAY

Another reason this is not a typical type of learning is that the pace is slower than we are used to. When I first got exposed to these psychological principles, somebody gave me three CDs by Dr. George Pransky, a master at teaching and training others in the Three Principles. I was instructed to sit and listen to them. As a Type A personality, I couldn't just do one thing at a time. I had to be multi-tasking or else it was a complete waste of my time. So I was exercising while listening to the CD.

I remember it like it was yesterday. He speaks really slowly. He was speaking in this dragged-out, slow voice, each sentence very distinct from the next one. My body was physically in pain from listening to him because it was so slow. When I finished this one-hour CD, I thought to myself, "I could have said that in five minutes! What is this guy's problem?" By the third or fourth time I listened to the CD, I was able to appreciate it.

Someone asked me, "Why would you listen to it three or four times if it was so painful the first time?" A valid question, I must say. My husband would tell you that I have FOMO: Fear Of Missing Out. Since someone I respect told me to listen to the CDs, I figured I must have missed out on something. I was motivated to listen to it again because I don't like to miss out. Little did I know that I had seriously missed out on something, and boy, am I glad I listened again. And again, and again.

Our minds can be compared to the engine of a car. When you gun it, the engine revs like a race car in order to pick up speed quickly. The RPM meter is there to tell you when the engine is revving at optimum speed. When we press the accelerator gently, the RPM meter reads 1 or 2. As we press harder and faster it reads 3 or 4 and starts to sound like a motorcycle. If you press the pedal to the metal, the meter flies to 6 or 7, and it sounds like the motorcycle is in your head.

I can relate to this because I was like that. My mind could go a million miles a minute, rehashing, replaying and repeating thoughts over and over again. There is a saying: doing the same thing over and over again yet expecting different results, is the definition of insanity. I was insane. I couldn't fall asleep at night because my mind was always racing. I talked so fast because I had so much to say and I was always thinking about what I wanted to say to you even while you were talking to me. I had no idea that I was using my mind against myself, and it affected my ability to function at an optimum level. We weren't designed to have our minds revving at high speeds all of the time.

Living in this busy mind, all I really wanted was peace, a sense of inner calm and connection. I didn't know that I was innocently thinking my way out of what I was looking for. As I learned about the nature of thought and how we are thinking beings, from cradle to grave, I started to realize that I was living my life listening to the running commentary in my head rather than being present in my life. I'm either living in my head or in my life.

Just as a car has an optimum revving speed that will allow it to function, last longer and not burn out, so too we have an optimum speed at which our minds work so we can function, last longer and not burn out. One thing I started to detect is that the speed I was living in was far from optimum, and I was feeling my engine burning out.

I can't say I slowed down overnight, but I headed in that direction. Eventually, I noticed I was no longer comfortable with being on the hamster wheel. I started to enjoy instances of peaceful quiet in my mind. The uncomfortable feeling of a busy mind was valuable information to tip me off to the fact that I was revving in my mind. The more conscious I become of this fact, the more freedom I have.

I did not know that when our minds are racing, it feels harder to hear our own inner wisdom and common sense. I had no idea that the reason I never thought slowing down was a good idea was because of a thought. I believed the thoughts, "Slowing down is a waste of time," "Slowing down makes me less productive," "Being less productive makes me less valuable," "Relaxed people are irresponsible, incompetent and lack integrity." Could you see why slowing down seemed like a bad idea to me?

Slowing down isn't meant to be good advice. It's the byproduct of an insight I had, one that made spinning out in a busy mind not look like a good idea anymore. I remember the day I had one of my first insights about the value of slowing down. Never before had I, in the middle of the day (or even at the end of the day for that matter), sat on my couch to read a book or a magazine. I didn't regard relaxing as a value when there was so much to do.

However, I decided to give myself permission to take a rest and relax with a book. I was sitting on the couch for fewer than ten seconds when my husband happened to come in the door from a meeting. I jumped up so fast to get busy. That's when it hit me: I'm not willing to give myself a respite because I wouldn't want my husband to think for a minute that I have it easy. My life was so busy with all the kids, cleaning, food shopping, errands, cooking and working that I didn't want him to walk in and see me sitting on the couch and think all of my complaining about being stressed out and overwhelmed wasn't true.

I was creating my own busyness because of this internal dialogue. I feel my thinking about what I think my husband thinks of me, and then I act out of this frantic feeling, running around all day without a second to pause.

I got a glimpse into the inside-out nature of life in that instant.

That glimpse settled my mind for a minute. As our mind starts to naturally settle, we sense life has slowed down. We think we are responding to the fast-paced life we live in and our minds are just a reflection of that life. We think we are observing reality when we look out at all we have to do. Really, our life is a reflection of our state of mind. As our mind slows down, we sense our lives slowing down. As our mind speeds up, we sense our lives becoming urgent.

As I started to enjoy slowing down and experimenting with a slower pace, I was pleasantly surprised to find that I was not less productive. Slowing down is not about being passive. A quiet mind does not imply inactivity. Surprisingly, I found that the less my mind spins, the more active I am. Imagine revving the engine of a car. The tires spin, but they have no traction. Slowing down allows you to get in gear so there is traction to drive. Disengaging from spinning allows us to engage in life with more perspective. I was actually more productive and more efficient because I was able to use my common sense as a guide rather than the constant chitchat in my head.

The interesting factor is that nothing changed. My environment, my circumstances, the things on my plate—they were still there, but I felt like I had all the time in the world to deal with them. It felt as if time stood still long enough to cultivate the moment rather than to have it fly by at lightning speed.

I know you want to ask *but how*? How do I get my mind to settle? The underlying assumption here is that there is something to change (i.e., my circumstance), but that's not always true. A settled mind is not a technique for creating change. Sometimes a quiet mind may just help you take notice that there is nothing to change outside. Although the answer may not land for you right now, please stay the course because I know it will. The understanding of where our experience of life is coming from will do the work for you without you having to do anything. Through insight and thought recognition, you will start to catch sight of something beyond what you already see, which will help you gracefully deal with your life.

To review, I made three points in this chapter. First, don't just stare *at* the illusion of life; try to stare *through* it, thereby allowing your mind to relax. Second, it would be helpful to be open to a different type of learning. Third, a slower pace provides an opening for our minds to settle, allowing space for life to be completely new and wonderous experience. So here we go; let's enjoy the ride!

CHAPTER 2

The Center of the Wave

OUR INNATE HEALTH

We are born innately healthy with peace of mind, resilience and a sense of security. Well-being is our default setting. We don't have to acquire anything. We don't have to work on ourselves or fix ourselves in order to become healthy and whole human beings. We already are; we just might not know it yet. Compassion, forgiveness, gratitude, serenity, inner peace, connection, clarity, joy: we are all of these things unless we think our way out of them. This is what I am referring to when I say our innate health. As our relationship to our thinking shifts, we begin to reveal our well-being more and more.

I realize some people may get bent out of shape

with that bold statement because we are so used to thinking that there is something wrong with us or with someone we know. We may believe that our well-being is only something that we visit, something that happens when we are on vacation or in the shower, but this is not true. Our health is a pre-existing condition, our birthright. We aren't broken and we don't need fixing. And neither does our thinking.

I remember reading that according to Jewish tradition, God sends a personal angel to each and every soul when it is a baby in its mother's womb, to teach the baby all the wisdom he or she will ever need to know. When he is born, the angel taps him above his lip, leaving the indentation mark called the philtrum, and he forgets everything he learned.

So I want to know: why bother teaching the baby everything he needs to know in the first place if he is going to forget it the second he is born? Good question, no? The answer is that navigating through this world can be daunting; nevertheless, as we travel on our journey, when wisdom is revealed, it feels familiar because we once learned it.

Within each of us is a path to the wisdom that we need to live our lives. God created us with emotional, psychological and spiritual well-being right now. Every morning in my prayers I say, "God, the soul you place in me is pure." It is never tainted. It can't be damaged, broken or diminished.

We each have a direct pipeline to a wealth of helpful ideas that can enable us to navigate life. Sometimes we call this common sense or intuition. The only thing that could block us from realizing our own innate health and purity is a thought: "It's not true." It is a very typical reaction to think, "I am the exception to the rule." You believe your circumstance is outside the realm of normal. Your situation is far worse than most. You are the only one on planet Earth who can't find their innate health or who may never have had it in the first place. I hate to be a killjoy, but there is no such thing. You are not the exception to the rule.

I know we all have thoughts at times that tell us we are broken, that our families are dysfunctional. We may be gripped by fear and self-criticism; entrenched in anxiety, despair and hopelessness; invaded by thoughts of insecurity, self-doubt and blame. The list is endless. However, the only reason we don't feel our well-being is because we get used to our habits and forget there could be something better. I am healthy despite my "dysfunctional" thinking.

My husband describes how he has lived for 30 years in chronic back pain. This pain has become his default setting, and after 30 years he had forgotten what it felt like to be pain-free. So if you asked him, he would tell you that pain is his default setting. In truth, though, it's not. It's just something he has gotten used to living with. When he experienced being pain-free and he tasted that for the first time in a long time, he realized there was a default setting under the pain. Once you sense the good feeling of being pain-free, it becomes easier to go back there and you want it more.

THE BUOY

When I say default setting, I mean we are naturally resilient. Envision a buoy in the water. Did you ever go to a pool where the kids are jumping on the buoy? They push it under the water and hold it there, but the moment they let go, it pops up to the surface. This is also the case with our well-being. Although I have a habit of thought that creates the perception that my health is blocked, covered, nonexistent or being pushed down...the instant I become aware that I'm the thinker and I'm creating that perception with thought, my health pops up, just like that buoy.

I don't have to psychoanalyze the buoy. As soon as the kids stop pushing it down, it pops up. When it feels like my calm state of mind has gone AWOL, I don't have to use my ability to think to worry about it or think it's a problem. The second I stop holding it underwater with a thought, so to speak, it will pop back up to the surface and begin to guide me again.

Our health is always available. It is like the sun. I may look up at the sky and see only clouds, but the sun didn't go anywhere. As soon as the clouds pass, the sun is there again. You might be thinking, "So if I'm not the exception to the rule, why don't I feel this health and wisdom you are talking about?" That is a valid question.

The simple answer is a thought. However, we are so entrenched in our own thoughts that we can't even separate ourselves from them to see clearly that we are thinking. The innocent misunderstanding of where our experience of life comes from is what trips us up. In order to understand this, we are going to look at universal principles that account for the entire human experience. A principle by definition is not a good idea, but rather a fact of life. For example, the principle of gravity is not a nice idea; it's a fact that we live with. Although there was a time in history where man did not understand how gravity worked, it didn't change the fact that there was a centrifugal force at play pulling everything toward the center of the universe. Once man understood this fact, he was able to use gravity to his advantage.

So too, there are principles that explain human psychological functioning: the Principles of Mind, Consciousness and Thought. We will discuss each one in the coming chapters. First, though, let's look closely at the way many of us perceive where our experience of life is coming from.

Circumstances ⇨ Feeling ⇨ Thinking ⇨ Behavior

My memory is that I was never an angry person until I had children. I would have completely convinced you that my upset, my anger, was because of my children. It looked so clear to me that the circumstances of my life (a chaotic home with four over-active little boys) was creating my upset. Their fighting made me frustrated, their defiance made me angry and their refusal to listen made me insecure in my parenting abilities. On the flip side, their cuteness made me happy, their successes gave me *nachas* (sweet pride) and when the house was clean for a little while, I felt accomplished.

Does this line of reasoning make sense to you? Most people believe that our anxiety, stress, fear or despair, as well as our happiness, excitement and satisfaction, come from the circumstances in our lives (i.e., our children, job, bank account, health, lack of health, etc.).

This points toward the misunderstanding of where our experience of life is coming from. We simply believe life is out there and it directly affects how I feel inside. If not for this "thing" in my life, I wouldn't be having these feelings. The belief is that "out there" causes my feeling state "in here."

If my worldview is that the world is coming at me, then my emotions are dependent on others. I'm stressed because I have a deadline to meet. I'm anxious because I don't know if I'm going to lose my job. I'm overwhelmed because I am needed by so many people in my life. So too, if I believe that my sense of calm and peace is dependent on something outside of myself, then if I don't have what I want—a marriage partner, a promotion, kids who listen, an emotionally available spouse, a psychologically healthy mother, a big enough house, my health—then it would make sense that inner peace and satisfaction is unattainable.

Here are more examples of how I saw life from this perspective:

- I'm happy when I get my way.
- I'm angry when my kids don't listen.
- I feel bored when I have nothing to do.
- I feel stressed when I have a lot on my plate.
- I feel peaceful when I'm at the beach or all the kids are sleeping.
- I feel content when nothing is going wrong.

That is how life looked to me and sometimes still does. That is how it looks to most of the world. Most people are wearing glasses that make the world look like their happiness or unhappiness is coming from out there, from someone or something else. Most people believe that the circumstances in their lives are what makes them angry, stresses them out, or alternatively, makes them happy, gives them inner peace.

I would like to stop here and have you reflect on some of the examples I gave. Have you ever had a different experience from what I described? For instance:

"I'm happy when I get my way." Have you ever gotten your way and still not been happy?

"I'm angry when my kids don't listen." Has there ever been a time where your kids didn't listen and you didn't get angry and yell at them to listen? Maybe you understood they were distracted. Maybe you were distracted with a friend at the park. Maybe you didn't take it personally that they ignored you, and you didn't get angry.

"I feel bored when I have nothing to do." Have you ever had nothing to do and actually enjoyed it—sat down, soaked it up and just appreciated the present moment?

"I feel stressed when I have a lot on my plate." Were you really stressed every minute or were there times when you forgot about the stress and just did the next thing?

"I feel peaceful when I'm at the beach or all the kids are sleeping." Have you ever sat on the beach with your mind racing a million miles a minute, unable to relax? It feels anything but peaceful, right? Or have your kids ever all been sleeping while you felt guilty for yelling at them and insecure for overreacting?

"I feel content when nothing is going wrong." Have you ever looked at your life and thought, "Everything is OK, nothing to complain about...so why am I so unhappy? Why am I bothered and irritated?"

I know I personally have undergone the gamut of what I just described. How is that possible? If my experience is coming from my circumstance, then the same circumstance should always make me feel the same way and you should also feel the same way as I do. If a circumstance objectively makes a person feel a certain way, then the whole human race should feel the same way when something happens.

Just because the majority of people react to tragedy in a similar way does not mean that the tragedy causes the feeling. There may be a correlation between the tragedy and how people feel, but that is not the same as causation. Each person's own state of mind influences how they feel about it. In a high state of mind, where trust and faith are strong, a secure feeling that there is purpose to this pain is a human response. In a low state of mind, where disconnection and anger are strong, blame is a human response. Going back and forth between states of mind is also human. How could someone have two polar opposite reactions to the same circumstance if the circumstance is supposed to create our emotions in the moment? It is definitely something to stop and get curious about.

What I am pointing to is that we have been trained by society to believe that our experience of life comes from our circumstances, from the "things" in our life that are either going right or going wrong. It's embedded in our language. "You are making me crazy!" "It's your fault!" We believe we are reacting accordingly, never stopping to ask ourselves if we are looking in an unhelpful direction. Looking "out there" to identify and describe what is going on "in here" is silly if you stop to think about it. It would mean we are all victims in life all of the time.

What we saw in this experiment is that sometimes we feel one way because of a set of circumstances, and sometimes we feel the complete opposite way from the same set of circumstances. Is the "thing" causing our feelings, or are our feelings coming from someplace else?

I am inviting you to reflect on each of these scenarios. Were we feeling our thinking at the time? At times our thinking may appear to be directly related to what is going on outside of us, but in reality it is only related to what is going on in your mind in the moment.

Our experience of life comes from our thinking 100% of the time. Realizing this fact—that every second my experience of life comes from within me, not from outside of me—is transformative in life.

So if we are open to taking off the glasses of:

Circumstances ⇨ Feeling ⇨ Thinking ⇨ Behavior

then maybe we can try on a different pair of glasses that enable us to see where our experience is really coming from. I'm not asking you to believe me, but to be open and experiment for yourself. Can you envision something beyond what you have been seeing up until now?

Thinking ⇨ Feeling ⇨
Experience of circumstance ⇨ Behavior

Our experience of life comes via our thinking. It is impossible to have an experience without thought. As we think, we instantaneously feel and then act out of that feeling state. Feelings are just thought in another form. It may appear to me like I am feeling your insult, or the upset of my child not listening, or the anxiety of my controlling boss, or any other circumstance that looks to me like that's the reason I'm feeling a certain way.

It's not true, though. We can only feel what we think. It's our thinking about the situation that we are feeling at any given point in time. In all of the previous examples, as our thinking fluctuated, so did our experience. Although it may look like it's the circumstances that have changed, if we dig a little deeper, we may see otherwise.

The key to healthy psychological functioning is the awareness of where my experience of life is coming from in the moment. The deeper I recognize the truth—that my experience is coming from within me, not from something outside of me—the more I reveal my innate health. The innocent misunderstanding that my experience is coming from something outside of me is what creates the illusion of lack of mental and emotional well-being.

The good news is, as a flash of awareness enters my consciousness, my health emerges—because it is innate; it never left. I may have felt like it was lost, but that is the illusion; it never really is. The human condition is that we all get lost sometimes, but being lost is different than not having well-being in the first place.

For example, if I never had a wallet in the first place, it would be delusional to think that if I wait long enough I will find my wallet. However, if I own a wallet and lose it, at least I know that I have a wallet and I just have to wait until I find it. If we never had well-being in the first place, then what I am suggesting would sound delusional, but what I invite you to look for is the truth: that we were all created whole and pure. If I don't feel my well-being, I may think I lost it. But if I wait, in time I'll find it—because it does exist. Well-being will always emerge if I don't innocently think my way out of it. How could I think my way out of my well-being? Let's talk about that in the next chapter.

CHAPTER 3

Go with the Flow

THE NATURE OF THOUGHT

There is a spiritual principle called Thought. There is a God-given ability to think that is different from the content that we think. The fact that we think is a gift. The *fact* that we think is different than *what* we think. Many people focus on what we think. They want to change, manage, fix or reframe their thinking, to make it more positive, paint it pink. They are focusing on the content after it has already been formed. I want to put our attention on the faculty of Thought: our ability to think, regardless of the content.

The nature of water in a river is that it flows downstream. Left to its own devices, it will continue to flow unless something, like a dam, tries to block the flow. So too, the nature of thought is that it flows. Left to its own devices, thought will continue to flow unless something, like my attention, tries to block the flow. If I don't hold on to any one thought with focus or attention, a new one will flow into my mind.

Have you ever sat near a beautiful stream, enjoying the calming sound of the water rushing over the rocks and the beauty of nature? Sometimes the water is so clean and clear; sometimes there is a piece of garbage floating down the river, maybe a beer can or a potato chip bag. Maybe tons of garbage float past, then the stream clears and fresh water passes by again.

Imagine two people sitting at this stream. One just enjoys the lush scenery, hardly noticing the things floating in the water, and has a peaceful sense of the stream. The other one gets bent out of shape and bothered that people could litter and ruin this beautiful public space. He can't stop thinking about all the inconsiderate people in the world who don't care about the environment. Instead of a peaceful experience, he finds sitting by the stream stressful. What is the determining factor of how a person is going to experience their time sitting by the stream?

The determining factor will be how much attention they give the garbage in the stream. For the first person, it basically went unnoticed; if he did notice it, he didn't make a big deal about it. For the second person, he couldn't get the garbage off his mind. As he paid attention to it, more thoughts about inconsiderate people filled his mind until he was feeling bothered instead of enjoying the stream.

Our minds are like the stream. Thought is flowing. Garbage may come, but do I have to pay attention to it? Imagine if you weren't so bothered by garbage, so interested in focusing on the garbage, and just waited patiently until the stream clears. Is that possible? Does the garbage have any power to upset our experience of sitting by the stream? Let's examine it.

What can a thought do to me? Here are some of the answers I got from a group of ladies during a seminar when I asked them, what power does thought have? What can it do to me?

- "So much power."
- "It could make me or break me."
- "It can affect me."
- "It can take me over."
- "Nothing."
- "I could act on it."
- "It could create a sensation in my body."
- "It could make me miserable."
- "It can control me."

Imagine I am writing a thought on a piece of paper and I'm putting it on a table: "*I'm not good enough!*"

What can it do to me? Can this thought jump up and attack me? Can it take over my body? Do the words on this piece of paper have the power to do that to me?

I am suggesting that a thought could come into your

mind and it can't really hurt you. No thought has the power to make you do anything or not do anything. You feel that thought in your body because feelings are thought in another form. In the next chapter we will discuss how our awareness of thought can bring it to life and create a full-blown sensation. But for now, can we remain open and curious and put it on the table? Can I detect a thought? Can I be an objective observer to the content in my head?

A strong thought habit, which is just another way of saying a recurring thought that a person thinks, usually feels true. When we look out into the world, we have no idea that what we see is really being influenced by the form thought takes in our mind rather than by what we are seeing. It's as if we look out into the world with tinted contact lenses on our eyes. Imagine wearing the contact lens of judgment and looking out at the world. Is it even possible to view life and not feel judgmental?

It reminds me of an old joke about an amateur artist who went to the Metropolitan Museum of Art. After looking at a famous painting he responded, "What is so great about this? It looks like a blob of yogurt! I can paint better than that." To everyone's surprise, he repeated this in front of many works of art, until someone said, "Can I have your glasses? You have yogurt all over your glasses." No matter what artwork he looks at, it will always look like yogurt.

The instant I get a glimpse into the nature of thought, this glimpse, this insight, allows me to see beyond what I am already seeing. For me, many times, it's the insight to be suspicious of my personal thinking. I may be duped into believing I am seeing the "truth" about life, when really I am seeing my own dirty glasses.

Here's a story to illustrate. The summer I was 13 years old, I had this camp friend, Kara, who was a pathological liar. Now, when I first met her, I had no idea. Those first couple of weeks she told the bunk stories that were amazing, spellbinding. Kara had us mesmerized. Then all of a sudden, we noticed things were missing from the bunk. We found out she was a kleptomaniac on top of being a pathological liar. Somehow she was caught with some of the girls' clothing and money in her cubby. When we realized she was stealing and lying, we were in shock. We realized that every story Kara had told had to be reassessed and looked at with a different pair of eyes.

Sometimes I feel like that with my thinking. I am noticing this pathological liar in my mind who tells me compelling and mesmerizing tales that look and feel so real, but I have to take them with a grain of salt. Just like this friend. Kara continued to tell us stories, but we didn't take them seriously anymore. Relating to my own thinking that way has given me a lot of freedom.

LIKE A FISH OUT OF WATER

Let's look at how thought works. A brain processes thought. Thought is not generated in the brain; the brain is a processor of thought. Here is an analogy. Your body is a food processor. Whatever you put into your body is what it is going to process. It's not going to judge or evaluate whether the food is a healthy apple or sugary candy (junk food, as my health-nut friend would say). Is my body sensitized enough to know the difference in the quality of food being processed? For some people, yes; for others, maybe not. We have the ability to desensitize ourselves by indulging in junk food more often than healthy food. My son often complains of a stomachache, but has no idea what he ate to create the pain.

I had a friend suffering from celiac disease, but she didn't know it at the time. Her stomach would hurt often. She had to strategically experiment to figure out which food she was processing that was giving her a problem. She kept at this process of elimination until she realized it was gluten. Once she had visibility to which foods were poisonous for her, she had the choice whether to eat them or not. Experimentation allowed her to get sensitized again. If she chooses to eat gluten, she knows what it will feel like in her body. It's not a mystery anymore.

Our brains are exactly the same way: they are processing thoughts all of the time. People can desensitize themselves to thoughts just like they desensitize themselves to food. If my brain, in any given moment, is processing healthy, helpful, wise ideas, my body will feel that type of thinking. If my brain is processing unhelpful, static, contaminated kinds of thought, my body will feel that type of thinking too. It's never about the content of what our brain is processing. Judging whether the thoughts are good or bad is not the point. The point is to be aware that our brain is processing thought like our body processes food. Our body's ability to process food is different from the actual food it processes.

Similarly, our ability to think and the content of what we think are two different things. As an analogy, imagine the faucet in your kitchen. The faucet carries water, but it is not the water. Any water that comes out of the faucet can be drunk, whether it is crisp and clean or unfiltered and contaminated with lead. Regardless of the quality of the water coming out of the faucet, the faucet remains a separate entity. What will determine how I relate to the quality of the water? Let's talk about that next.

CHAPTER 4

The Tide Rolls In and Out

THE NATURE OF CONSCIOUSNESS

There is a spiritual principle called Consciousness. Consciousness is the ability to be aware of thought. It's the ability to give life to a thought, to give us the full-blown motion picture experience in 3D. Meaning, I have the ability to take a thought and animate it, bring it to life and make drama out of it. I can make a mountain out of a molehill, make nothing into something. Just by fueling the fire, I can create my own movie. We can all be drama queens (or kings).

As an example, here's a story that I remember from my childhood about my father. He had vertigo. As a cameraman for ABC Eyewitness News, he sometimes had very interesting stories to cover. One day a jackhammer fell and killed someone at a construction site. He walked onto this plank to take a video of a crane that was going to show how the accident happened. After he had been recording for a few minutes, his partner yelled out, "Gary, I thought you were afraid of heights?" He looked down and froze. He had an expensive camera on his shoulder. They had to send two guys out to get him back. One minute he was fine, the next he was paralyzed. The circumstance hadn't changed. He's out on the plank videoing with no problem. Then, wham—paralysis! What happened? Once he became aware of the thought "I'm afraid of heights," he immediately experienced that thought as fear and paralysis like a full-blown movie.

Here is another example of taking a thought and making drama out of it. My husband opened the fridge and said, "We are out of milk." A benign comment, a statement of fact. But I was able to take that comment and create a world or drama around it with thoughts such as, "I'm such a bad wife, how come I'm not more on top of things, he thinks I'm incompetent, I am incompetent." Could you imagine that from five short words, "We are out of milk," I spent the rest of the morning reeling about how horrible I was? This is the power of Consciousness in action. Once I become aware that I am the director, I can call, "Cut. Take two."

It's like my client, Rebecca, once told me: if my toe hurts because it is being pounded with a hammer, the instant I realize that I am the one holding the hammer, I can stop hitting my toe. If I think the pounding is coming from someone else, then what can I do? But if I see that I am the one doing the pounding, I don't have to keep doing it. I am the thinker, but I am not my thoughts.

A RISING TIDE

Imagine Consciousness as a glass elevator going up and down. It can go as low as the basement or as high as the penthouse.

To explain what it feels like for a person who is in the basement, try grabbing your face with your hands covering your eyes, as if a monster is attacking you. You can't fathom there is anything beyond your hands. There is no perspective. In the basement, we are extremely limited in our vision and we take everything very personally. Everything is about me: they are doing this to me, they are talking about me, they are looking at me, it's my fault, etc.

From the basement, we feel despair and hopelessness as our minds spin out of control. It's very dark and black. Suicidal thoughts, destructive behavior and using our drug of choice each seem like the only option. No matter what thoughts we have, from the perspective of the basement, everything will look and feel hopeless and impossible, desperate and depressing. Everything is very heavy. For example, having a benign thought such as, "I have to hurry or I'll be late," while in the basement will feel like the world will end if I'm late, everyone will hate me, everyone will notice. It's all about me and there is pressure and stress. I can't take it. I will lose my job, I'll be out on the streets. I can't be late, yet I can't move. I feel paralyzed. What's it worth anyway?

As the glass elevator rises to the lower floors, envision your hands pulling slightly back from your face. Now they are right in front of your face rather than grabbing your face like a clawing animal. Your perspective is limited and constricted, but it does shift from having no perspective at all. Your awareness opens slightly, but it is still subjective. Your thinking still has a grip on you, but there is a little bit of space. Possibilities don't seem impossible, just highly unlikely.

From lower-level floors, rushing around like a chicken without a head while yelling, "Let's go, we are late!" and knocking people over to get where you need to go will look like good ideas. Your thoughts look true and it would be hard to believe they aren't. The thought "I have to hurry or I'll be late," will feel urgent and compelling. It will feel like a problem if you're late for carpool or to a date or to a meeting. You will have concerns about disappointing others and what they will think of you if you're late.

As the elevator rises to higher floors, move your hands to arm's length out in front of you. Your awareness and perspective becomes expansive. You don't take things personally; you intuit the bigger picture. You have more objectivity. The possibilities are endless.

From the penthouse, acting calmly, keeping your

wits about you and accessing your wisdom in the moment look like good ideas. You don't take your thinking so seriously; it doesn't have a grip on you. You feel light regardless of your thinking. The thought "I have to hurry or I'll be late" will be taken in stride; it won't feel like "the truth," but like a passing idea. You will feel confident and secure in the fact that you will get to where you need to go in the right time. You will also have a better chance of accessing any good ideas or wisdom to help make that happen in a calm, pleasant and timely fashion.

Where many people get stuck is in their expectation (thought being brought to life via consciousness and feeling as if it's true). We are "supposed to" be in the penthouse all the time or we aren't "supposed to" be in the basement right now. We innocently keep ourselves on lower levels of consciousness with our habits of thought. The thoughts of "It shouldn't be this way," or "It's not fair," or "I should be doing better than this," or "It's a problem that I'm here," are all examples of personal thinking filled with expectations or judgment that come with feelings of bother, annoyance, anger or frustration.

In this level of consciousness, it will look necessary to blame yourself for not doing a "better job" with your thinking, as if that were possible. It will seem normal to blame your state of mind on something outside of yourself rather than to wait for your mind to settle and let the system self-correct.

SETTING THE COURSE

A typical analytical question arises: "How do I do it?" The question implies that our states are meant to be managed or controlled. If what I am about to say sounds frustrating, try to notice whether the frustration is coming from your thoughts or what you are reading. This approach is not here to teach you how to control or manage your states of mind, your moods or your thinking. (If you are asking yourself, "Then why in the world did I buy this book?"—hang in there with me.) There are many techniques and methods in existence meant to do just that. However, that's a different ball game altogether.

Imagine you're on the court playing basketball and someone comes along with a football and asks you, "How do I make a touchdown? Do I throw the ball through the hoop?" This would sound absurd to a sports-oriented person. Sweetie, you're in the wrong game. The football field is outside. In here we make baskets, not touchdowns. It's just a different ball game.

My personal experimentation has taught me that the ball game of trying to manage and control my thinking requires a ton of effort with very little reward. In that ball game, the question, "How do I do it?" might make sense, but it is based on the faulty belief that we are supposed to be able to get on top of, fix, reframe and control our thinking.

I am inviting you to look at a different ball game altogether. In the ball game of understanding, our state of mind is not meant to be managed and controlled, just understood. What are we understanding? How the system works. How our mind works. That the system self-corrects. As it self-corrects, I realize I am feeling my thinking. At that time, my consciousness rises and my health surfaces like the buoy. My feeling state will change as my thoughts settle down. This is the doing which really is a non-doing: allowing the mechanism to self-correct rather than sabotaging myself by aggravating the waters of my mind with more thoughts about it.

Have you ever seen a snow globe? You shake it up and the snow fills the waters and covers the scene in the globe. Within a minute of putting it down, the snow settles to the bottom, the water becomes clear and the cute winter scene appears again. That is how our minds work. The content of the snow is irrelevant. I am not interested in evaluating if the snow is good or bad. If we shake it up, so to speak, we agitate the waters of our minds. If we become a traffic cop in our heads, evaluating our thoughts, we inadvertently agitate our minds. Letting the snow settle and letting the waters of our minds settle allow clarity to emerge.

Let's ask a different question, then. How can my understanding of Thought and Consciousness guide my navigation of the natural ups and downs of life more gracefully?

REFLECTIONS OF THE WATER
I was a film major in college. If you can remember

back before VHS and DVD, we used film to record movies. In order to watch the movie, a reel of film was loaded onto the projector and frame by frame, the film would pass over the projector lens. As long as the projector was plugged in, once you flipped on the projector lamp, whichever frame was passing over the lens would show up on the screen. As the film rolled, another frame would be projected onto the screen every millisecond. It happened at such a fast pace that it appeared like continuous movement rather than individual frames.

In the film projector analogy, the reel of film is Thought and the projector light is Consciousness. Without the light, we wouldn't see a movie on the screen even if a reel of film was passing through the lens. So too, without the awareness of a thought, we would not have an experience of it.

The content of the film is irrelevant. Whichever reel of film we load will pass frame by frame over the projector lamp, where it will be illuminated and then projected to play out on the screen of life. We literally project our thoughts onto reality like a projector projects a film onto a screen.

In a movie theater, we may forget we are watching a movie for a period of time. We may scream or cry or laugh, but deep down we have some awareness that we are in a movie theater. No matter what film is being shown on the screen, we know it's a movie. In our own minds, though, we can lose the clarity that we are the creator of our experience. So we sometimes get scared when we are by ourselves with our own thoughts. However, if we focus on how our minds work, on the fact *that* we think rather than on the content of *what* we think, we might not get so scared. As thought passes through the lens of our mind it will be projected onto our screen of life. What we see will be our own personal reality, our own private viewing—always.

That being the case, whatever content is being viewed will be brought to life via this system. We will feel all of our thinking as instantly as we think it. If we can identify the mechanics of how it works, we don't have to be so afraid of or bothered by the content. Like the river, the film of thought in our minds is always flowing. In the next moment, there will be another thought projected onto our screen of life and we will feel that thought in real time.

It's helpful to know the mechanics of how thought works. If I don't grasp the mechanics, it makes sense to believe every thought I have is true since it feels that way. I mean, come on, who would think something that is not true? That seems like the craziest idea I have ever heard. At one point I started realizing: wait a minute, my perceptions of life, my interpretations of actions and my judgments of things are sometimes off. There are times I am missing information or not seeing the whole picture, yet I relate to all of that thought (perceptions, interpretations, judgments) as if it were true. How is it that it feels so true?

Thought feels true in the moment when I am tripped up by the misunderstanding of where my experience is coming from. When I know clearly that my fear or anxiety is coming from my thinking, I take my personal thoughts with a grain of salt. However, when I think my fear or anxiety is coming from something "out there" in my life, I take my thoughts quite seriously, feel justified and then react from that place.

There's a story of two rabbis who hear a plague is coming. The plague is guaranteed to make everyone in the city insane. One rabbi says to the other, "Let's each put a red dot on our forehead, so that when the plague comes and we gaze at the dot, we will be reminded that we are insane." Meaning, I may not be able to stop the insanity, but at least I can have some awareness that I am insane and not take it so seriously.

Understanding how thought works points to a deeper mechanism at play: the mechanism of free will. Knowing that I can use my thinking to create an unsolicited drama or to wait for clarity gives me the ability to access my free will. Without noticing how I can create illusion through my own thinking, my level of free will is compromised.

Examples of thoughts that look true are:
☞ He did hurt me.
☞ My parents did abuse me when I was a child.

- I really was bullied.
- The boss really did take the credit for my idea.
- My child really was disrespectful.

I am sure all of these things happened, but I am only experiencing them in a certain way because of the thought I am having now about the situation.

I am not implying painful things do not happen in life. I am not taking anyone's experience away from them. The pain is real pain; we feel it in every fiber of our being. I am only pointing toward the shift that can occur as our state of mind changes. By no means do I want to minimize someone's pain, trauma or difficult times. I only want to point us towards an awareness of how we are going to experience our pain, trauma and difficult times. It will always come via our thinking in the moment about our life's circumstances. The relevant question is, if I were in a different state of mind, would I have a different perspective and experience of life?

NAUTICAL NAVIGATION

God created us with the most sophisticated biofeedback system, a GPS to let us know the quality of our thinking in the moment. We don't have to be hooked up to monitors and wires. Our bodies feel our thinking. No matter what content is coming through our mind, we will feel it.

So how will I know when I am being duped without

getting caught up in the content of what is duping me? My feeling state is a good gauge. It lets me know the level of consciousness I am in by the quality of my thinking (i.e., whether it is impaired or not, or whether I have perspective or not). By feelings, I don't mean emotions; I mean a physical sensation in my body. The feeling state is an indicator to let me know how trustworthy and reliable my thinking is in the moment.

I want to make a big distinction here. I am not distinguishing between good and bad feelings. I am not saying certain feelings are good and certain feelings are bad. The distinction I am pointing to is being able to distinguish reality and illusion. My level of consciousness is a good indicator as to whether I am being duped into believing an illusion or whether I am perceiving reality with clarity.

On lower levels of consciousness, while thought looks and feels real, our perspective is skewed. Our content is not trustworthy and reliable because we are living in a virtual reality of our own making, an illusion. On higher levels of consciousness, we take our thought in stride. Our perspective has clarity which allows us to envision something beyond our self-created illusions. This content is extremely trustworthy and reliable. At higher states of consciousness, we are closer to touching the Oneness of the universe.

When the biofeedback machine is giving me messages of tension, frustration, tiredness, tightness, agitation, anger, sadness, distress, hopelessness, compulsion, urgency, anxiety, stress, overwhelm, insecurity, annoyance, bother, vengeance, resentment (did I cover them all?)—this is good information. It lets me know that the spiritual pipeline called Thought has been hijacked and that a septic tank has just leaked garbage into my brain. Don't drink the water! And if you do, don't be surprised if you get sick.

Meaning, that on a low level of consciousness, although we believe our thoughts are true, our feeling state—the sensation in our body—can guide us to question the validity of the thoughts we are having at any given time. These feeling states are a guide telling me that I am using my ability to think to cover up my soul, my innate health. It's not thinking I want to trust. I don't want to take my thinking too seriously, be too interested in it or respect it because I'm living in muddied waters right now. There is no judgment here. There is only the recognition that the quality of my thinking is low and I don't have the perspective I need when I'm in the basement or in low levels of consciousness. There is no problem. My awareness of where I am will guide me insightfully to wait for my well-being to surface.

Once I am aware that I am feeling my thinking rather than something else, this thought recognition is all I need to allow the system to reset itself. The system is designed to self-correct. I don't have to do anything to make that happen. That is what happens when I don't get in the way by blaming my circumstances and making everything personal.

If I am feeling anxious or stressed out, I don't have to be so bothered; it's not a problem or a statement about my competence. It just is what it is: I am feeling an anxious or stressful thought in the moment. If I wait for my mind to settle, a wiser, more helpful or productive thought may come to guide me...or not. But a settled mind will feel better no matter what.

It's like carrying a 50-pound weight around and then putting 25 pounds down. Even if you don't get a great idea about how to find someone else to carry it for you, it still feels better to carry only 25 pounds instead of 50 pounds. It's helpful to know that access to wisdom is available in an instant. We may not always hear it, but it is always available and we can learn to listen for something wiser, deeper and more helpful more of the time.

When the biofeedback machine is giving me messages of calmness, security, presence, gratitude, connection, serenity, warmth, relaxation, freedom, lightness, acceptance, balance, peacefulness—you get the picture—this is good information as well. This feeling state, these sensations in my body, lets me know that the spiritual pipeline called Thought is clear and trustworthy, and that wisdom is most likely flowing through.

At these times, I really want to be listening. I trust the wisdom, use it to guide me, respect it when it comes and feel grateful for it. This wisdom has also been called insight, common sense, the guiding voice from within and the sound of our soul, among other things. This is the voice that I don't want to accidentally or intentionally override.

The more of a connoisseur I become to the feeling states of thought, the more free choice I have as to whether to believe or dismiss the content of my thinking. Said another way, the more clarity I have about my state of mind in the moment, the more free will I have to disregard my personal thinking. When I am less interested in my personal thinking, I feel better and I tend to get in less trouble. Most problems (I'm tempted to say all) occur because a person is in a low state of mind and doesn't know it, but believes their thinking to be true and then acts based on that feeling. Unfortunately, following that wave of thinking can leave lots of damage and pain in its wake.

I want to be very clear: These are generalizations. There are times when a "negative" feeling could be wisdom, such as the feeling of being manipulated or feeling unsafe. So too, "positive" feelings, such as feeling calm, could be mistaken for complacency. It's not the content of the thought which is of value, but where it is coming from. What state of mind are we in when we are thinking it? Is it coming from ego or my essence? My body or my soul?

In summary, when a new idea is flowing through you, it has a feeling and guides you well. When an old, repetitive, used up thought is flowing through you, it also has a feeling and can guide you. In my experience, I've had insightful wisdom show up about my old repetitive habits, guiding me by saying, "Don't act right now. I know the compelling feeling seems like the truth, but hang on for the ride."

With time and experimentation, as our familiarity with our feeling state deepens, the natural byproduct is that we spend less time living in a busy mind. And when we do find ourselves spinning out, it doesn't seem to last as long. Navigation, to me, looks like this: when I am in the penthouse, I am really grateful and enjoy riding the wave of connection, security and inner peace. When I am in the basement, I usually let the uncomfortable feelings pass through me as I ride the wave of disconnection, insecurity, fear and anxiety. One might feel nicer in my body, but the other one is not a problem, just a part of being human.

When we are in the basement, we may not be able to stop our thinking, but as our awareness about the nature of thought increases, our experience in the basement shifts. It's not the same basement anymore. Once our relationship to our thinking changes, we don't experience the basement in the same way. A child may be afraid of his own shadow, but once he realizes it's his own reflection and not someone chasing him, it's unlikely he will continue to be scared of it.

So too, once we realize it is our own thinking, it makes it slightly more difficult to take it so seriously. Our thinking doesn't have the same power, the same intensity. It loses its grip. The downs don't feel as bad as they did when we took our thinking really seriously, and they don't last as long. On some level, the jig is up, the game is over—

you can't pull one over on me in the same way as before I had any awareness. The thinking can't have the same effect because we don't relate to it the same way anymore. That is freedom.

If it is true that I can only experience a feeling because a thought passed through my brain, then a thought passing through ("This is too hard" or "I can't" or "This isn't fair" or "He's wrong") will be my reality, always. It doesn't really matter what "it" is. My experience of "it" will be "hard", "I can't," "it's not fair" or blame. However, if that thought were to lose its grip, if my consciousness were to go up, I would see "This is too hard" as a thought and the feeling may dissipate. I could then look out at my life and see and feel something completely different.

The elevator is going up and down all day long. That is called the human experience. My level of awareness and consciousness is fluctuating moment to moment. My moods go up and down independently of the circumstances in my life. I don't have control over this any more than I have control over my thinking. There is good news, though. There is always another wave coming, always another thought available. Am I open to it? Looking for it? Listening for it? Where does it come from? We are going to talk about that next.

CHAPTER 5

Beyond the Horizon

THE NATURE OF MIND

There is a spiritual principle called Mind. Mind is the infinite energy behind all of life that we call God. Again, using the film projector analogy: the reel of film is Thought; the projector light is Consciousness; and the electricity, the energy source that powers the projector, is Mind. Without the projector being plugged into the wall, the reel of film and the light are literally powerless. It is energy that powers the whole system moment to moment, the power source behind our ability to think and the level of awareness we have of our thinking at any given time.

Is it possible to look beyond the limitation of what is already visible to you right now? Most would say no.

Unless you know where original thought is generated. This type of thought is called an insight. It comes from the depths of our souls. An insight is not something I can manufacture, no matter how hard I try to use my intellect to manufacture it. It's something that comes from beyond my finite mind...it comes from the Infinite.

Just as my heart beats without my having to make it happen, just as my next breath comes without my having to make it happen, my next thought comes without my having to make it happen. I am not the creator of my thoughts, but I am the thinker of them. I've seen relief, freedom and empowerment on people's faces when they hear this. I've also seen fear, disbelief and frustration on people's faces when they hear this. My state of mind will determine my relationship to this fact.

The relief comes when a client, who has lived in extremely hateful self-talk or immense resentment about someone else for so long, gives themselves permission to stop beating themselves up for having such horrible thoughts. They were not the creator of those thoughts. There is no place for guilt if they did not create the initial thought. The freedom comes when they don't have to believe those thoughts anymore. The empowerment comes when they know that even if they continue to think those ugly thoughts and bring more of them on inadvertently, it doesn't have to mean anything about them or their character.

THE COAST GUARD

Imagine you get a cut. You can put on hydrogen peroxide and a Band-Aid, but you aren't the one making the healing happen. The healing—allowing blood to coagulate and scabs to form—begins instantly by a Power way beyond you. It's only when I get in the way of the healing and start picking at the scab that the process gets impeded. But if I let my body do what it was created to do, then it will heal itself because of the God-given immune and healing systems with which we were created.

So too, we were created with a God–given psychological immune system. Meaning, if I get a "mental cut," the healing will begin immediately unless I start picking at it and impede the process. This psychological immune system is my default and will self-correct with what I need in the moment if I let it. Just as my body informs me when I'm sick by the symptoms of fever or nausea that show up, our body informs us when our minds are "sick" by the "symptoms" of uncomfortable feelings that show up. At some point, we realize that our thinking is headed in an unhelpful direction, and that realization is the psychological immune system in action. That flash of thought recognition is your wisdom piping up. It's the self-correcting mechanism you were created with that will guide you back to your essence, your soul and your innate health.

THE ENDLESS SURF

An insight, a person seeing something for themselves from within, is where change occurs. It's not self-created. It is offered up to us as a gift from the infinite Source of all thought, God, who is sending wisdom to us constantly. We all experience insight; we just might not have paid much attention or given it the respect it deserves. It tends to be simple, a quiet whisper, sort of like an *aha* moment. Maybe we notice something about a behavior or a pattern that we didn't see before. Maybe it's a simple "Don't do that," or "I can," or "Wait." Once you see it, you're changed. You don't have to work so hard to listen to it because you believe it and it makes sense.

We have all heard stories of someone who's tried to quit smoking. They slowly decrease their intake from two packs a day to one pack a day to twenty cigarettes, until they are down to two cigarettes a day and they just can't pull the trigger. Then we hear of someone else whose uncle died of lung cancer and boom, they quit, just like that. How is that possible? The second person got an insight from within, and a shift occurred. Smoking didn't look the same. It just didn't look like a good idea to smoke anymore. They didn't have to work at it; the insight did the work for them. That's an example of the God–given psychological immune system at work, providing healing without effort. At least, not the kind of effort we're used to.

Usually, when we think of effort, we think of a lot of self-control, willpower and focus. The mentality is that it's all about me. We live in a lot of personal thinking about how we're going to make change happen. It tends to feel like a lot of work with little return. Ego thinking does not create sustainable change, but insight does.

The instant a thought pops in, it has a feeling that comes with it. When an idea, a thought, wisdom or a helpful direction is being piped into our brain, there's a feeling that comes with it. You feel like you're on top of the world, like you can manage. You could be stuck in a situation that is really difficult, and you get an idea and you think, "Wow, I can do this. I can handle this." Yet, the thought didn't come from you, but from something beyond you.

Have you ever had someone come to you for advice and you found yourself saying all the right things? After reflecting back, you thought to yourself, "I don't even know where that came from, but gosh, that was really good." You didn't create it yourself, but it kind of just popped into your mind. Another example of a thought that just pops in our mind is "Don't forget your keys." You couldn't have forced yourself to remember the keys, but you're really grateful that the thought popped in just in time. It's an effortless effort.

This effortless effort is more like stepping into the God–given stream of consciousness that is flowing through my mind and being open to catching it, to watching it, to letting it move me. It's about trusting that it will guide me to greater heights than all my personal ideas about how to make change happen. The flow is always coming. Sometimes we hear it, sometimes we don't; but we can orient ourselves toward it.

The place we are orienting ourselves toward for the peace, security and serenity we seek is the unknown, because God is found in the unknown. Quite ironic, no? We spend our lives trying to be in the known, wanting to control the outcome, yet seeking inner peace and a spiritual connection which cannot be found in the known. It is only when we stop being a backseat driver and acknowledge that God has the wheel, that we are actually filled with a sense of security. In Hebrew, the word for security is *bitachon*, which usually gets translated as trust. When we trust that God's got our back, the feeling of security fills our body and we are present to the unknown. The unknown is another way of saying the energy behind life, the endless array of different possibilities of thought that could be available to us. It's the place where miracles happen, the place of hope, passion and unlimited potential. This is the place where God resides.

If I saw this deeply, I would not fear the unknown; I would embrace it, desire it, realize that the wisdom I am seeking to live my life is in it. Truth be told, every waking second we are living in the unknown. We just delude ourselves into thinking we're not. "Doing" gives people a false sense of security and control. They can delude themselves into thinking that they can know an outcome if they do something about it.

It's not in the *doing* where change occurs. It's in the *being*: being open to an insight that can guide you in what to do and show you how to do it effectively. It is being in a state of mind where trust naturally shows up, where you are able to trust that you will get what you need when you need it. It is being able to trust that if you are not getting a fresh thought, that is also what you need at the time. Being has a feeling to it: a fluidity to life that we get to be a part of. Doing, has a feeling to it: a tense urgency of trying to control the outcome, getting it to be my way.

The unknown is counterintuitive. The exact thing we fear is the place where all of our answers lie. We need fresh, insightful thought to blow out our stale, habitual thinking, yet we fear the place where this unique thought originates. A new thought is by definition unknown, something we never thought before.

Imagine if my relationship to the unknown shifted. What if it weren't a problem to be in the unknown? What if the unknown is exactly where my answers are found? What if I could trust that I will get what I need in the moment I need it and if I don't have it yet, I'm OK? Could this insight change my reality?

As my relationship to this unknown place recalibrates from one of fear, control and disbelief to one of trust and letting go, I feel my point of free will rise.

CHOOSING TO ENTER UNCHARTED WATER

Each time I choose to look toward the unknown rather than toward my personal thinking, I strengthen the free will muscle. Jewish sages say, "In the way a man wants to go, he will be led." If I choose to want to receive fresh new thought by orienting toward this Divine space, there will be a tipping point where the universe will comply and send me more of it more of the time.

Even before my exposure to the Principles, I already believed that we had free will at all times to create our lives and impact the world around us. Through the Principles, I gained a deeper appreciation of the mechanics of free will as well as greater access to it. Most of us think that our decisions begin really close to the point of action: don't yell at your husband in front of the kids, don't binge on the whole chocolate cake, wait patiently for your turn to check out at the grocery, get out of bed instead of pushing the snooze button.

What the Principles illustrate is that our free will is impacted much earlier, in the arena of thought. If I live in certain habits of thoughts about myself, or about others in my life, my behavior during the course of the day can almost be predicted ahead of time. It will be like a reflex, apparently without thought, hence the word "habit." I tend to say people don't have as much free will as they think they have.

Meaning, if someone has a temper, without any awareness or consciousness of his thinking, he may not yet have the free will not to yell. However, with heightened awareness that he is feeling his thinking, at some point, he could have an insight not to believe the thought that is telling him he must be angry and yell in order to get anything done. At that point of insight, his free will may shift. In these kinds of situations, if we're not aware of where our habitual, reflexive behaviors are coming from, we don't have that much free will to make different behavioral choices and decisions.

As we become more aware of the role thought plays in our lives and we get a bit more visibility about our previously "hard-wired" beliefs about life, all of a sudden we get greater access to choice in these areas of life. This awakening process provides a greater sense of freedom. It's one of the things that feels pleasant about gaining understanding of your thinking; you feel less tight, less constrained, as if the straitjacket that was life just opens up into a whole world of possibility and choice. The result is more access to my free will, to my ability to truly be the creator and initiator of my life instead of feeling like the victim of my life.

If you are thinking, "That all sounds nice, but why is that not my experience?" Why don't I feel like I am accessing insight to increase my free choice? Maybe this self-correcting psychological immune system you mentioned isn't working within me? Can mine be defective?" If the thought "I am the exception to the rule" crosses your mind and you believe it, that will be your experience in the moment.

Another typical question I am asked is, "If all thought comes from God, then why would He give me such unhealthy and unhelpful thoughts? Is He out to get me? Does He want to hurt me?" It's a big topic that books have been written about, and this isn't the place to address why in depth, but I will briefly touch on it from my perspective.

The fact that the world was created implies purpose. According to Jewish thought, the purpose of the world is to give man pleasure. The ultimate pleasure is to be in a relationship with the Creator Himself. As we have mentioned before, the feeling that comes when we are tapped into Reality, Truth and our soul, is one of presence, hope, calm, resilience, joy, compassion, forgiveness, connection. This is true pleasure because it is emulating the Creator Himself. The spiritual pleasure of connecting to Reality is greater than any physical pleasure. It's greater than any delicious chocolate, any thrilling adventure, any relaxing vacation, any physical touch.

The universe is constantly broadcasting wisdom. Are we listening? Are we aware of it? Do we hear it? Yet in order for a human being to have free will, the universe also has to be broadcasting something other than wisdom. It's like the radio. Radio waves exist, and the channel I tune into will determine whether I hear beautiful music, the news or static. This is the internal struggle of every man: to distinguish between reality and illusion. The Principles help explain this struggle by describing how consciousness brings all thought to life, regardless of whether it is reality or illusion.

For example, I was keenly aware of my own internal struggle of wanting to be able to control my temper and not to get so bothered when things weren't going my way. Yet I felt like I kept failing. There is a profound, yet simple piece of Jewish wisdom that says, "Turn from evil and do good." But I didn't know how to practically follow it—before I understood the Principles. Now I see it is not referring only to the realm of action, but to the realm of thought as well. There is an internal human battle between our good inclination and our evil inclination. These are two forces inside of us and they both use thought to create our experience.

Evil and good are not judgments here, but rather expressions of different realities. We are being advised to turn away from unhelpful, illusory thoughts that lead to behaviors we tend to regret, and turn toward the wisdom, the space where all possibility lies. Once we know how our minds work, we can use them however we want. The choice is ours. The actual thoughts we get are not up to us, but the choice of where we want to orient is completely up to us. Every time we are gifted to see beyond the temporary illusion our thoughts create, we step into a beautiful space.

Prior to gaining perspective, our habitual thinking can trick us. However, with visibility and perspective, we trust that our wisdom is being guided by a Force bigger than us. With experience and experimentation, this trust grows and we find ourselves naturally choosing to orient toward the true Source of health and change: the universal broadcast.

I have personally found that it can be so easy to fool myself into thinking I have received wisdom. Since the urgency isn't as intense as it used to be, I've fooled myself into believing I was in a healthy state of mind when visited by the thought "I'm right," as I responded to someone's email or text. However, in hindsight, I saw that if I had waited for my mind to settle even more, I'd have seen something deeper and less subjective. "I'm right" didn't really matter, and once it passed there was no need to say anything.

The good news is, I have become accepting of my humanity and the mistakes that I make. I know there will be times when I will be duped into thinking I am accessing my inner wisdom. It is at these times that I am truly grateful that I can utilize the Torah as an objective guide to God's wisdom.

THE SOURCE OF WATER

As Arnold Patent said, "We don't create abundance. Abundance is always present. We create limitations." The Jewish definition of God is that He is the source of all blessing, the source of all life. When we make a blessing, it always begins "Blessed are you our God...." The word for blessing in Hebrew is *baruch*, from the word *breecha*, which means a pool, a source of water. We are saying that You, God, are the Source of everything. The Source by definition is abundance, which means the source is always present. The only reason a human being would not sense that abundance, that Source, is because they are using their mind to create limitation.

We are living in the feeling of our thinking, which can create limitation. But it is only a mirage. If I have a thought, "I feel disconnected," or "I don't feel God in my life," or "God doesn't love me," or "There's no hope for me," then it is a no-brainer why I feel disconnected, lonely or hopeless.

There is no more reality to my feelings than the thoughts I am having in the moment. In a low level of consciousness, any content will look and feel real, creating my personal reality. But if I am open to the possibility that I create limitation, that my thinking is unhelpful and is not something to respect or take so seriously when I am in the basement, then I can let the self-correcting mechanism with which I was created do its thing. As my mind quiets and my level of consciousness goes up, my relationship to those types of thought will shift on their own, leaving space to feel a connection that exists innately.

I may be blessed with a rise in consciousness or an insight that allows me to deeply see that I am believing the mirage, that it doesn't really exist but for in my mind. The thoughts then won't look and feel so real. In the penthouse, abundance is clear, present; we are tapped into it, we encounter the blessing and the gift of life. Through the gift of thought, this infinite Power created us with free choice, with the ability to choose the direction we want to orient toward. Do I trust that this infinite Energy is working through me and guiding me? Do I listen for it? We'll discuss in the next chapter what listening for wisdom feels like.

CHAPTER 6

The Sound of the Sea

THE POWER OF LISTENING

Have you ever taken your kids to a baseball game? The first time I did, they brought their mitts. I was thinking, "What are the chances the ball is going to come? And if it comes at 90 miles an hour, what are the chances you are going to catch it?" Yet, they come, mitt in hand, because they want to be prepared. If it's going to come, they want to be ready. This is my stance on life: if wisdom is going to come, I want to be prepared. I want my mitt; I'm ready. My mitt in this analogy is my curiosity—being curious and open to the possibility that something else might come into my mind.

Being prepared is about listening from a place of curiosity rather than from a place of certainty. What do I mean by a place of curiosity? I mean a place of openness, pondering, wondering, reflecting or thinking in a way that we don't usually do. In other words, not a place of analyzing, trying to figure it out or processing. Do you feel something happen in your body when I say the words analyzing, figuring it out or processing? It feels tense. You can feel your eyes scrunch up like you are focusing really hard, like your mind might explode unless you understand what you are trying to figure out.

Do you feel something different in your body when I say the words openness, pondering, wondering and reflecting? Can you feel what being curious feels like, what being open and reflecting feels like? It's like opening your hand from a clenched position. It's like being able to catch something that's falling, like a snowflake, without thinking you're creating the snow. It's being receptive rather than reactive. Can you feel the difference? Holding my mitt means my hand is open, ready to receive rather than control. In this space, miracles happen.

When our minds are filled with tons of content—stressing about how the weather is going to affect our plans today, analyzing what to do or what to say, replaying a conversation we need to have, thinking about our job, what we need to do, how bad we feel, our problems, our habits—we tend to stay focused on the content. We get very interested in our content and listen to our thoughts all day long. If I spend the whole day listening to the content whirling around in my brain, then it's no wonder I feel lousy and not present in my life.

Imagine a scenario where you are at work and the radio is playing in the background. There are probably times where you hear it and are bothered that you can't concentrate. There are probably times where you forget it's even playing. How many people walk in their home and turn on the television right away? At some point it becomes background noise and they don't even pay attention until something loud or vivid grabs their attention. Have you ever been on a plane with a baby crying? For a while, it is all you can think about, but at some point, you forget about it and move on. We all have areas in our life where there is background noise, but we somehow manage to block it out at times. So too, the chatter in our heads can become background noise, where we lose interest in it and stop focusing on it. So if I'm not listening to the chatter in my head, what am I listening to?

First let's ask: what is listening? What am I listening to? What am I listening for? Is listening being able to regurgitate back what someone said? Is listening being able to give good advice? Is listening something I do to be a good friend? Can a person listen if their head is already filled up with so much other stuff?

As our mind quiets down, our emotional well-being emerges. We become open to listening for wisdom. Although there may be thoughts on my mind, I don't have to be engaging them, focusing on them, dancing with them. I could be present with who or what is in front of me, listening with less on my mind. I could be listening for something other than what is going through my mind, something novel, different—something deeper. I could be listening *for* life, rather than listening *to* my habitual thought track.

THE EYE OF THE STORM

Another word I like to use to describe listening is "*presence*." There is a feeling that comes with presence. A vitality, an aliveness, a centeredness; like an intimacy with myself or someone I'm with. When I am present to life, I am fully engaged in the moment. I am tuned in to life rather than caught up in the distracted feeling many of us have for most of the day. This connected feeling naturally shows up when a person has less on their mind.

What does it mean to be "present"? Everyone is talking about "mindfulness" and being in the moment. We all know what it feels like to be in this zone, but we don't know how to get there. The truth is that there is no "there" to get to. We are here, in the zone, right now, but for our thinking that creates a different experience.

In Judaism, one of the names of God is a conjunction of the verb "to be": I was, I am and I will be. Being implies presence. God just is. When you are in touch with "what is"—Reality—you are present and it feels good. The Principles help us disengage from a virtual reality of our own making so that we can connect to the true reality.

Human beings have the free will to be able to use

this gift, this ability, to think and to feel their thinking in order to bring them closer to Reality or further away from Reality. The beauty of the gift is that it was designed to bring to life whichever direction a person chooses at any given point. Therefore, our personal reality is created by our thinking, regardless of its veracity.

Now, many people don't like to call it Godliness. Maybe they call it the oneness of life, the infinite energy behind life, the life force or universal energy; but whatever they call it, they are pointing to something beyond the human being. When we tap into that, we are tapping into the highest state of consciousness. In that state of mind, where our ego thinking has no grip and I have less on my mind, the feeling of presence emerges from within my soul.

On the other hand, as the ego thinking grips me, I feel a distancing of my soul as the pain of mental distress. Since life is moment-to-moment, I could feel present one second, then feel overwhelmed by the thoughts in my head the next second and be back in the feeling of presence a second later. There is no judgment here, just a human being—being human. However, an awareness of my state of mind in the moment enables me to listen for something deeper than the chatter in my head, which will guide me to navigate life with more grace.

The closer a human being comes to recognizing Oneness and piercing beyond our personal separate realities, the more presence shows up. The natural byproduct of coming in contact with the presence of Godliness is that we have less on our mind, allowing a sense of security and well-being to bubble up. So too, the natural by-product of blocking the presence of Godliness with a world of ego-oriented thought allows for a sense of insecurity, anxiety and hopelessness to surface.

ROCKING THE BOAT

What would block me from listening, from being present? The only thing that takes me away from the moment is a personal thought or having a lot on my mind. Regardless of the content or the form it shows up in, any thought that seems more interesting than what is in front of me right now takes my attention away from the present. It's like being at a baseball game with a running commentary in the background; you could forget to pay attention to the game itself because you're so distracted by the commentary.

Nonetheless, most people are not even aware that they are thinking beings, so they don't realize their minds are full of thought. Most people assume they are seeing reality and would say their personal thought has nothing to do with it. For example, what happens if you ask a person looking at a glass filled with 50% liquid whether the glass is half full or half empty? Whichever answer they give, they probably assume their perception is the truth. We don't even realize that what we see is not "truth," the real information, but is rather a reflection of our state of mind and the feeling state we are in.

We tend to listen from a place of misunderstanding that fact. Imagine you are trying to share a problem with a friend but, unbeknownst to them, they live in personal thought. They believe what they think about your problem is the truth. It would never occur to them that their state of mind is influencing how they are reacting or behaving. If a person has a lot of personal thought that it is their responsibility to help you solve your problems, then when you talk to them, they don't really hear you. Instead, they are listening to all the thoughts they are having about the responsibility they feel to help you, and they will try to solve your problem by giving you good ideas about how to change, what to do or how to fix it rather than really listening to what you have to say.

Have you tried sharing a problem with someone who has a lot of judgmental or critical personal thinking? As you're talking to them about your problem, they may be telling you what you are doing wrong, why it should have been done another way, how it would have been better if you had done it this way or how unfair it is that you have this problem in the first place. They are judging and critiquing instead of listening.

Have you ever spoken to someone who lives in a ton of self-conscious thought? No matter what you share, somehow the conversation is always about them. How they can relate to your problem because of a time they had that problem...and then they continue to share about themselves. They unintentionally make everything about them, even if it has nothing to do with them.

What about someone who listens from an anxious habit of thought? You want to share your concerns about your job and they keep answering you with what-if scenarios: "How are you going to manage?" "What if you can't pay the bills?" "What if this or that happens?" Are they listening to you, or are they listening to their own anxious thinking about what you are saying?

Have you ever bumped into a friend in the supermarket who asks how you are, and as you start to answer (because you assume it is a close friend after all, not just an "I'm fine" acquaintance), you notice she is checking her texts, scanning the shelves for an item or checking her watch? This is an example of living in a distracted habit of thought. This habit comes with a fragmented feeling. Your friend feels compelled to listen to all of her to-dos instead of listening to you. Of course, your friend has no idea that she is doing this and it is nothing personal against you.

It is human nature to view life through our personal filter, our habitual thinking...until we don't. Once I become aware of a habit of thought, it doesn't have the same grip on me, which gives me more free will. Often, it becomes easier not to listen to it or believe it. The thought recognition alone, the flash of awareness, provides the clearing. As my mind settles, two amazing things happen. First, I become open to listening for something new beyond my habits. In this new space, there is room for God's wisdom to bubble up inside of me. I can then rely on the new wisdom inside of me instead of habitually focusing on what I already know about their problem (i.e., how they should be doing things). Second, I make room for another person to have their own space so their own wisdom can guide them.

I am always asked for specific ways to help people quiet their minds because they want to be more present and to be able to listen better to themselves, to others and to the messages that the Divine offers up moment to moment. The one thing that most practices, such as mindfulness, meditation, CBT, positive thinking, affirmations, etc. have in common is that they offer techniques to quiet the mind. The understanding I am pointing toward is different in that regard. There are no techniques. The understanding itself is what quiets the mind. In my opinion, it's been with far more success and less effort as well.

ANCHORS AWAY

Many of us use analysis to try to figure out how to quiet our minds. Analysis is like a power tool. If I need to hammer in a bunch of nails in the most efficient way, I will use a nail gun. But the nail gun does not take into account whether the nail is straight or crooked. It just does its job, and it does it very well, I might add. We want to make sure we use the tool properly. With a straight nail, analysis can powerfully unleash reality; however, with a crooked nail, analysis may bring us to live in unnecessary pain of our own making.

There are many reasons we choose to use our analytical skills (the key word being "choose"). There are also times we don't actively and consciously choose to analyze, we just fall into doing it out of habit. What if all of our intellectual analysis is not as helpful as we thought it was (at least not in every situation)? We are so habituated to analyzing—what we are doing, why we are doing it, how we are doing it, where are we doing it—that we don't even grasp how the process of analysis could potentially be blocking us from what we are looking for in the first place: answers, clarity, understanding. If we do see it, we would view the process as something to respect.

We live in the faulty belief that we figure things out or gain insight through the process of analysis. Innovative, creative ideas and clarity are not self-produced through our ability to analyze or use our intellect better than others. They come as gifts from something greater than ourselves. The sooner we realize that truth, the easier it will be to let go of our habit of analyzing things to death.

This is not to imply that analysis is bad or that it is a process never to be used. The question is: am I doing it out of habit, or is it called for in this situation? Analyzing, trying to figure something out, is only helpful when you have all of the factors at play. If that is the case, then making a pros and cons list and figuring out which decisions to make based on the analysis is appropriate.

When I don't have all the factors and I am only

speculating, I find analyzing becomes spinning, trying to grasp the unknown factors which cannot be grasped and then being frustrated that I can't make a decision. From a place of spinning, the answers that are readily available may not be heard.

When you find yourself struggling to figure it out so much that your face starts to scrunch up, it's a good idea to take a break. Working harder to understand is taking you in the wrong direction. Gaining a deeper understanding of the Principles behind human psychological functioning is not going to come through your personal ego thinking. It will come as a gift, an insight, a new thought that you never had before which enables you to peer beyond your present view. It's a spiritual revelation that comes in God's time, not yours.

We don't need to work so hard. I'm not suggesting that you turn off your intellect, but I am suggesting that your common sense will guide you if and when analysis is necessary. You don't have to continue to use it out of habit. The more visibility we get, the less habitual we are in life, and when that happens we have more free choice to use our feeling state to guide us. I don't want to analyze because I was programmed to do it; I want to use that skill because I am choosing to.

Understanding the Principles reveals many facts that, when seen insightfully and deeply, quiet the mind. It reveals the fact that we are all thinking beings and the content of our thinking is not a problem (there is no need to change, fix or reframe our thoughts). It reveals the fact that our thinking is ever-changing (the reason we don't need to change, fix or reframe our thoughts). It also reveals the fact that we are living in the feeling of our thinking (the reason there is no need to fear any particular thought, because it's just a thought we feel; nothing more, nothing less). A flash of insight, the momemt of thought recognition, is the instant our essence is revealed. When we see the fact that we think, our relationship to our thinking shifts and the byproduct is psychological freedom.

PART II

THOUGHT STORMS

Habits of Thought that Visit Us

CHAPTER 1

The Ripple Effect

WHAT IS A HABIT?

What is a habit? After looking in the dictionary, I came across the following definitions. 1) A recurrent, often unconscious, pattern of behavior that is acquired through frequent repetition. 2) An acquired behavior pattern regularly followed until it has become almost involuntary. Both of these definitions discuss behavior. But behavior comes after the fact of thought. Instead of looking at habitual behavior, I'd like to look at what is behind habitual behaviors: habitual thoughts. We call being continuously visited by certain thought content a habit of thought. Some of our habits of thought can feel like "thought storms."

Habits of thought visit us in many forms and flavors. Many times, we are not even aware we are thinking in the first place. We may live in a prison of our own making without our awareness or choice. As we gain awareness of the fact *that* we think, not just *what* we think, there is an adjustment in the way we relate to our thinking. Our habitual thought patterns and the thought storms that visit us take on a different meaning, allowing us to view them in a new light. This new light, this fresh perspective, is what creates effortless change. When we perceive thought differently than we did before, or insightfully see thought in a less-personal way, change is simple.

Our minds can trick us into believing our habitual thinking: that a certain circumstance is creating our feeling, rather than a thought in the moment. However, when that thinking becomes visible, voluntary and conscious, it slows down enough for us to notice it as thought. We are then reminded that our feeling state comes from within us, not from a circumstance.

The goal of this section is to help you notice the fact that you are experiencing your life via your thinking. Another term for this is "thought recognition." The second I realize that I am "in" thought now (i.e., creating my experience of life via my thinking), I have a flash of insight, a jump in consciousness, which helps me discern my thinking for what it is: personal thought. From this perspective, I don't have to be so taken with the dialogue in my mind, leaving me more time to live my life.

My husband came up with a great analogy: there is

a difference between being a player on the field and being a bystander in the stands. When we are interested in all of the content in our minds (whether the flavor of the day is expectations, judgements, self-consciousness, anxiety, insecurity...), we are bystanders in the stands, living in feelings of disconnection, insecurity and distress. From this level of consciousness, all thought looks and feels real.

The instant of thought recognition is an *aha* moment. "Oh right, I'm in the stands now. Let's get back in the game." On the field we are living life—feeling present, connected and peaceful. Being in the game is only a thought away.

Nevertheless, being in the stands is not a problem. I am not teaching a technique to control or manage your thinking so that you never end up in the stands. Being in the stands is part of being human. We will never be free of that. Healthy psychological functioning can be defined as recognizing where we are at any given moment, whether we are in the stands or in the game. That realization is real freedom.

Mental and emotional distress can be defined as the feeling that occurs when we are living in the misunderstanding of where we are in life: when we are in the stands, but we think we are in the game. The following chapters are meant to awaken us to habits of thought that keep us in the stands. The deeper our understanding, the more free choice we have to notice when we are in the stands and when we are in the game. When we trust that our internal psychological immune system will reset and self-correct, we allow our innate health and inner wisdom to guide us.

CHAPTER 2

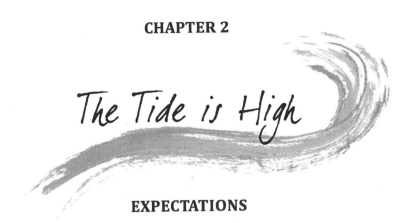

The Tide is High

EXPECTATIONS

Personal thought can be tricky because we don't usually recognize it for what it is. Some examples of personal thought are:

- My cleaning help needs to show up on time.
- My husband should remember my birthday.
- My kids shouldn't wake me up if I'm sleeping.
- I deserve a bonus for my dedicated work.
- Why is there traffic now?
- My bank account should never go below X.
- I need eight hours of sleep in order to function.

I am sure some of these "shoulds" look really true to you, and you could probably find a bunch of friends who would agree. These beliefs (hidden or not-so-hidden) create an expectation of how life is supposed to go. We honestly don't see our beliefs as an assortment of thoughts that we decided were true.

We think our circumstances, our version of reality, is true, and we don't have any visibility to the role thought plays. Truth be told, you are not feeling the distress of your cleaning lady not showing up, your husband forgetting your birthday, being woken up by your kids or your boss ignoring your efforts. You are feeling your thinking *about* these scenarios. When we wake up to that, we can make the choice to lower our expectations, hold on to them or throw them out the door. There is nothing wrong with holding on to them. Some expectations may be quite appropriate. I am trying to bring to your attention the fact that the distressed or disappointed feeling comes from our expectational thinking. Whether that feeling is justified or not is irrelevant.

Expectations can also be layered with judgment (i.e., more thoughts that we probably don't even realize are thoughts). Some are:

☞ Life should go this way, not that way.
☞ It isn't fair.
☞ You shouldn't be late.
☞ I'm not living up to my potential.
☞ I should know better.
☞ I should have more self-control.
☞ I should be in a better place than I am.

- This is a problem.
- I don't deserve this.
- What were you thinking?
- I can't handle this.
- I have too much on my plate.
- You shouldn't treat me that way.
- My kids should get good grades.
- My kids should listen and behave.
- My washing machine should last 10 years.
- I should be married already.
- I was supposed to have kids already.
- Marriage was supposed to look different.
- It shouldn't be this hard.

These are typical thoughts that visit most of humanity. Most of us look out at life and think our opinions, perceptions and interpretations are accurate. We never stop to notice the state of mind we are in when we are thinking about life. As an analogy, let's imagine we're looking out a clear window with the intention of observing the world with proper perspective. Yet, in front of our eyes, unbeknownst to us, is a curtain. Sometimes the curtain is opaque, sometimes sheer, but it always obscures our vision—and we don't even know it. We believe we are looking out a window with a clear view.

This curtain is the form our habits of thought take. In this example, our habit is expectation or judgment. I look out at life and think I am observing the truth, when in reality, all I am seeing is my version of it. That version is filtered through the judgmental thoughts roaming around in my mind. I get lost focusing on the curtain instead of peering past the curtain, past my personal thinking, to the bigger picture of life.

I have a son whose curtain was "life's not fair." It seemed to him that he was always the one to get in trouble. He felt like he was always the one blamed for the disturbance, sent out of class or yelled at for instigating his siblings. His reality was that he was extremely unhappy, and he wasn't aware that thought had anything to do with his unhappiness. He was looking out at life through the curtain of "expecting" (that life should go a certain way) and "judging" (when it didn't go that way). He then blamed his circumstances for life not meeting his expectations. It would seem impossible for life to be anything but unfair. He couldn't grasp that his unhappiness was directly related to the feeling that comes from the thought "life's not fair." He even said to me once, "Mommy, are you trying to tell me that I could be happy even if life's not fair?"

This idea was so foreign to him at the time that he couldn't even begin to imagine that his relationship to his thinking about "unfair" could shift. If he hadn't expected life to be fair, then he wouldn't have been bothered when it wasn't. He couldn't see that he was feeling the pain of his expectations.

Most of our discomfort and disillusionment comes from our thinking rather than from life itself. We inadvertently create quite a bit of our own suffering, because we are caught believing that things should be different. The pain we feel in those "should" moments is the gap between reality and what we expect reality to be. The bigger the gap, the more self-inflicted pain.

When we feel bothered, self-righteous, inconvenienced, stuck or annoyed, these are good indicators that we are feeling the effects of our judgmental thinking. Naturally, from this restricted state of mind, the way we act toward others will probably be nasty, snappy, blaming, controlling or hopeless. We are all familiar with the blame game. From the basement, it usually looks like my unhappiness is someone else's fault.

The moment of thought recognition—an insight telling me that I am feeling my thinking in the form of expectations or judgments—brings me back to life and out of my head. As I lose interest in that daily dialogue inside my head, I feel better. I can be OK with the "is-ness" of life, rather than my expectation of what the "is-ness" is supposed to look or feel like.

When I let go of expectations, I experience what really is: I am present. Present to the Divine reality beyond my pettiness, which serves life up to me exactly as it should be in this moment. As my perspective shifts, somehow the questions of blame and fault aren't in the equation. The judgments, negativity and expectations now look illusory. If I need to make amends or rectify mistakes because I acted out while being visited by low-quality thinking, I will insightfully know what needs doing and how to do it. In this Divine presence, acceptance, forgiveness, compassion and clarity naturally appear. It's not something I have to force myself to do; it's who I am. Have you ever noticed that when you let go of expecting how something should be, you are pleasantly surprised that you are OK with how it actually is?

CHAPTER 3

ANXIETY AND STRESS

DROWNING IN ANXIETY

Anxiety is just another form that thought can take. When we don't see the inside-out nature of life, we tend to blame our circumstances for creating our anxiety. We tend to think, "I wouldn't be anxious if my husband weren't late, if I knew my child was safe, if the mortgage would go through, if the test results were good, or if I didn't have to make this life-altering decision with major ramifications."

To us, it really does seem that we wouldn't be plagued by anxiety if these situations didn't exist (i.e: if I didn't have to worry about money or make this decision, I'd be fine). Most of the time, it looks to us like the money or the decision is creating our angst. We assume we are thinking certain thoughts because of our low bank account or our lack of clarity. In truth, we can only feel our thinking, not a circumstance.

If our minds are filled with what-ifs and concerns and we focus on them, then we will get more of those thoughts. Plants live on water. Animals live on food. Thoughts live on attention. Once we feed our thoughts by paying attention to them, all of their friends and relatives jump on the bandwagon. Before we know it, our minds are housing a whole neighborhood of anxious thoughts, and we are wondering why we feel anxious.

The next question most people ask is, "How can I not feel anxious about not having enough money or making a big decision with serious ramifications?" It is true that there are natural consequences to not being able to pay the bills. There are consequences to any major decision. Nonetheless, our experience of the path we take is not determined by our bank account or the actual choice we make. It is determined by the thinking we are having about our bank account or our choices, moment to moment, as we walk down the path.

From the penthouse, with perspective and a deep feeling of connection to the Divine, we can walk down any path with grace. From that perspective, the thinking that naturally shows up will produce a contented, secure, trusting feeling. Only from the basement are we plagued with judgmental thoughts ("It shouldn't be this way." "It must be the wrong path.") or anxious thoughts ("What if I can't pay?" "What if I lose my job?" "What if it's the wrong path?"), and then we feel judgment and anxiety in our bodies. There is good news: *who cares?* If I recognize that anxious feelings are an indication of low-quality thinking, not worthy of my respect and attention, I can let myself be in the feeling and trust it will pass. It's just a thought wave I am riding. I can let the wave flow through my body and out my toes. When it passes, so will the feeling. I can hang on for the ride.

I can hear some of you shouting, "But what if I really can't pay my bills or it really is the wrong decision?" Instead of answering that, I have some questions for you. What if not being able to pay your bills isn't actually a problem? What if the feeling of lack is created by our thinking, not our bank account? What if life is not about making the right choices, but about experiencing whatever unfolds regardless of the path you choose? We only fear not having enough money or making a wrong decision if we have a false belief (another thought) that life is about making money or making the "right" decisions. What if our premise is misguided?

What if the question isn't, "Did I make the right decision or the wrong decision?" What if the question is, "How can I best navigate life regardless of the bills I have to pay or the decisions I have to make?" If this sounds too idealistic for you, let me ask you this: what's the alternative? Would you rather hold on to the notion that not having enough money or making decisions is a problem?

When our relationship to our thinking about money and decision-making shifts, so does our feeling state. True, we will still have to figure out how to make enough money to pay the bills. Yes, we will still have decisions to make daily. The question is: if we want to access our own wisdom, and we want helpful ideas about how to do these things, what state of mind would be most helpful?

We tend to think our free choice lies in the actual decisions we make. This may not be the whole picture. Our decisions are only as good as the state of mind we are in at the time we make them. If we are not gifted with a higher level of consciousness at the time, then our decision is limited to the perspective we have in the moment. Can we be open to the possibility that as our perspective expands, which it naturally does, our anxiety may decrease on its own? Our free will may be to wait for our perspective to change, rather than to try to stop our anxious thoughts and feelings.

I am suggesting that our free choice may be in another realm altogether. Is it possible that we spend too much time focusing on the outcome, rather than focusing on the process? Focusing on the process here means understanding that we are the thinker, and being open to getting glimpses of what *that* means.

The question is not, "How do I stop my anxious thoughts from coming?" The question is, "What is my state of mind when I am doing my thinking?" The anxiety in my body offers me vital information that, if I am willing to listen to it, will guide me. It is telling me that the quality of my thinking is low, unreliable. If I don't feed it attention, thought will flow like a stream, and something different may flow through. If nothing comes, I can also be OK having anxious thoughts pass through my mind without needing to change them or take them too seriously. Many people are visited by anxious thinking; that in itself is not a problem.

Believe it or not, it's our relationship to our anxious thinking that creates most of our pain. Thinking about our anxiety creates more anxiety than the original anxiety. If we gave ourselves permission to feel whatever comes through the system, it would be over before we know it, like a scary roller coaster ride. Instead, we unintentionally add more thinking to the mix: "This is a problem." "Why don't I have more faith?" "There is something wrong with me." "I'm going to die." No wonder we continue to feel anxious. When we think a particular thought is a problem, we unwittingly keep that thought in play.

I had a client, a high school-aged girl named Sara. Sara had started having panic attacks. She came for a couple of sessions and stopped having the attacks. What happened? Sara had no idea that the panic attack, that gripping fearful feeling, was coming from a thought. It wasn't a statement about her character that she was being visited by these thoughts. She wasn't a bad person for having them. It was just a habit of thought that she was focusing on over and over again.

Once Sara understood the nature of how panic attacks work, it took the fear out of the equation. Once she let go of the self-judgment, she gave herself permission to be OK with having a panic attack. She saw that she was just feeling her thinking in the moment and she realized that having a panic attack comes from thought. It didn't mean Sara was guaranteed to never have one again, but she wasn't scared of them anymore. Her relationship to the panic attack shifted, as did her relationship to the thinking that brought on the attack. Even if she were to have one, her experience of it would be completely different because her thinking about it had changed. The change came insightfully, not because she worked hard to change or reframe her thinking. She no longer felt bad or wrong for having certain thoughts or feelings.

Sara saw for herself that thoughts can create a panicky feeling, but if she waited it out, it would wash over her. Whether it washes over in a minute or in an hour or in a day, it will always wash over because no one can hold on to the intensity of a thought forever. I remember Rabbi Chaim Levine telling me that a client with an eating disorder once told him the compulsion to eat lasted forever. He asked her to time it the next time she had a compulsive craving. At their next session he said, "I'm curious, how long was forever?" "Seven minutes," was her reply.

STRESS, A LIFEBOAT?

Stress is another example of a form that thought takes which creates a feeling of being anxious and overwhelmed. There is a belief (thought) that stress and adrenaline make you work faster, help you reach your deadlines and motivate you positively. Many people think, "If not for stress, I wouldn't perform/ be on time/ study/ meet my goals/ be successful/ make my deadlines." Isn't it interesting that we even call it a deadline? No wonder we feel stress about it. Imagine the shift that might occur if you just started relating to it as the due date that it is. Notice there is a difference between time pressure and stress. It may be true that there is a due date, but that doesn't necessitate feeling stressed out in the process of completing your work or making a decision on time.

One thing is for sure: if you think stress is necessary, that will be your experience. You will feel stressful thinking in your body and attribute that urgent, rushed, high-strung feeling to your success. I bet being around you when you are performing, studying or being successful must be really fun...not!

Besides valuing stress, we also tend to habitually think our stress is coming from our circumstances, that is to say, from all of the things we each have on our plate. Truth be told, our stressed-out feeling is a reflection of our stressed-out state of mind. For example, it looks like our busy schedule stresses us out, our disorganized house stresses us out, our lack of work—life balance stresses us out and our mother-in-law stresses us out (although not mine). However, the only reason we see our schedule as busy and stressful is because of our state of mind.

If we were to experiment, we might notice that at times, when our minds have quieted down, we also feel that our schedules aren't so crazy. The catch is that we can fall into the trap of thinking, "Well, that's because I had less to do today." We could miss that it was a shift in our state of mind that created a calmer experience of our schedule, rather than the number of items on the list. Even if you are convinced that the stressful feeling comes from something outside of you, I invite you to look again. It is only possible to feel stress if you are having stressful thinking.

For instance, have you ever had a lot on your plate—a long to-do list, a due date, a timely decision to make—and you felt really stressed out, but for a second you experienced a break in the stress? Is it possible that the due date wasn't on the forefront of your mind for a moment? Maybe you were interrupted by a friendly phone call, maybe you stopped to help a colleague or maybe you remembered fun weekend plans. Whatever the reason, in that instant, the stress left. On some level, you gave your-self permission not to have it on your mind. Instead, your focus was your phone call, helping a colleague or thinking about the weekend.

How is it possible to have a minute without stress if the situation of having a lot on your plate, a deadline or a decision to make is what is stressing you out? The plate is still full, the deadline still exists and the decision hasn't been made. But for a moment, you weren't focusing on it, and in that moment, your feeling state shifted. Now, it may shift back the moment you start focusing on what a problem it is that you still have so much to do. That would just indicate the fact that once you started thinking about the situation again, you felt stressed again.

When we do what we need to do, without all of the thinking and commentary surrounding it, we are able to handle what we need to do without making it worse. It's no wonder we feel so overwhelmed when our minds are layered with thoughts like, "I shouldn't have so much to do," "It isn't fair," "I'm never going to get it done," "Someone else should have to do it," or "I can't take it." All these thoughts come with feelings that have nothing to do with the to-do list.

Am I willing to experiment with my to-do list today without all the thinking about the to-do list? Is it possible to get through all of the things on my plate from a place of calm, presence and security? If not, can I at least acknowledge that my stress is not coming from my to-do list, my due date or my decision, but rather from the stressed-out thinking I have about all these things? (Which is not a problem either, it just signifies more thought.) What if a relaxed state of mind produced productive and creative results far beyond what I think is possible in a stressed mind?

Feeling anxious, panicky or stressed comes from thoughts running through our minds, and our bodies feeling the impact of those thoughts. There is nothing wrong. There is nothing to do. There is no need to change or control or manipulate anything. Just noticing we are feeling our thinking and realizing we don't need to strengthen the feeling with added layers of habitual thought can be helpful. And if we do add layers of thought, so what? It's all part of the human experience. Give yourself permission to be human.

CHAPTER 4

Dead in the Water

STAYING IN WHAT I KNOW

We have been trained in school and by society to compartmentalize, to fit things into what we have already learned in order to make sense of life. For instance, if I take a parenting course, I tend to listen to the instructor while trying to fit the new information into what I am already doing. Although many of us want to have an open mind, we tend to habitually react to life and then wonder why we couldn't do it differently.

In physics, we understand that we can't be in two places at the same time. So too, we can't have two thoughts at the same time. If we are focused on what we already know, how could we hear something new?

Learning something new, even the ideas in this

book, may or may not sound similar to a lot of things we have already learned. There is no problem with that. They may be the exact same ideas; they may be totally different. What I invite you to be open to is the possibility that an original thought is always available if we are not focusing on an already-formed one. A new thought may provide another perspective on what we already believe. Even if something we already know is true, even if it's helpful, there may be a deeper truth below the surface.

How much more so when we are focusing on something that we already "know" which is not true? What about those times when our limited perspective or our misinterpretation becomes our "truth"? We learned that thought can look and feel real. So if we think we know, it looks and feels like we know—even when we don't perceive the whole picture. If that is the case, then we may believe there is nothing new for us to see. When we realize for ourselves that our thinking can trick us, we are humbled and don't buy our thinking so quickly.

For example, I had a client, Rachel, whose daughter, Dina, pushed her buttons big time. Their relationship was quite volatile. Don't we all have that one child who forces us to take a parenting course? Most people take the parenting course because they think there is a problem with their child and they want the expert to fix it. Their mentality is, "Here, fix my child and then I'll be happy."

Rachel believed that her child had a problem. Every time Dina behaved defiantly, Rachel felt defeated. She couldn't get close to Dina because she found her so repulsive. Any interaction they had was constantly tainted by Rachel's habitual judgmental thinking and expectations about how Dina should behave. Focusing on the thought "my child is the problem" limited the possibility for a different thought to come.

Without a new thought, an original idea or a fresh perspective, we are locked into an old, familiar way of being. Both mother and daughter unintentionally got locked into this dynamic. Neither one could see beyond her perception of the other one. An insight has the potential to change the relationship.

Rachel experimented for a while. As she became more aware of her thinking, she saw how compelled she felt to react to her daughter's behavior when Rachel was feeling extremely upset. She began to notice that her feelings of insecurity and anger were coming from her thinking about Dina and not from Dina's actual behavior.

One day, something happened. Rachel was in a good mood, and Dina did the same defiant thing as usual. This time, however, Rachel actually thought it was funny. That was an eye-opener for her. Another thought came in when she wasn't focused on what she "knew," which was that her daughter was the problem. She thought, "That's funny." She had never found Dina endearing before, but in that moment, she did. As Rachel continued to experiment, she began to notice that when she focused on how repulsed she was by Dina's behavior, it didn't occur to her that Dina could be endearing. As her mind quieted, there were more times where she found Dina endearing and enjoyed her presence, and was less annoyed by her behavior.

Here are some other examples of how our thinking limits us. I "know"...

☞ how wrong they are.
☞ how incapable they are.
☞ how irresponsible they are.
☞ how inconsiderate they are.
☞ how controlling they are.
☞ how they always insult me/ embarrass me/ hurt me.
☞ how much he loves me.
☞ how amazing this prospective job is.
☞ that I'm dating the perfect guy.
☞ what good advice I am giving or getting.
☞ what the truth is about life.
☞ that this is a good investment.
☞ what an appropriate action to take is.
☞ what the right thing to do or say is.

It's helpful to notice that locking ourselves into viewing life and people in certain ways, whether for the good or the bad, can at times block a deeper truth. There is always something else to grasp beyond what I think I "know" in this moment.

I also don't mean to imply that we can't trust ourselves. The question I've asked before is, who is talking:

my essence or my ego? What state of mind am I in when I believe my thinking? What is the feeling state in my body when these thoughts are passing through? Living in content that I have already thought many times (ego thinking) creates a feeling in my body. It has a bit of self-righteousness about it, an I-know-better feeling. Being open to something else and hearing my inner voice tell me something I haven't thought before has a whole different feeling.

This feeling state can guide our listening as well. Have you ever listened to a friend complain or gossip? When listening, did you focus on how she always complains about the same thing and seems to be the straw that stirs the drink? It is irrelevant whether you agree or disagree with what she is complaining about. Are you aware of your own habits of thought as you listen? Do you make judgment calls about whether her complaints are justified, or listen with half an ear because you have decided she is the "complainer," "negative one" or "gossiper" in your group?

What if we let our feeling state guide how we listen? Let me explain what I mean by that. Can I distinguish the feeling of internal calm and peace from the feeling of being disturbed or annoyed? If I am feeling bothered, then I don't want to be taking my thinking about my friend too seriously. As my feeling state changes and settles down about this person, can I listen with fresh ears, without assuming I "know" who she is or what she is going to say? It would be interesting to try listening with curiosity and see what thought shows up. We might be pleasantly surprised.

CHAPTER 5

Water Under the Bridge

LIVING IN THE PAST

What is a memory? Memories are experienced as thought in the moment. Simply stated, a memory is thought in another form. We have the ability to bring our pasts into the present via our thinking. Since I feel my thinking in the moment, if I focus my thoughts on a past event, it will feel as if it is happening right now. Whether I am remembering a pleasant event or a traumatic one, I have the ability to think about a memory and bring it to life in the present. Sometimes this can be pleasurable; sometimes it can be quite painful and even destructive.

Incidents that happen to us in childhood can constrict us for our whole lives if we aren't aware that they don't have to. I had a client, Talia, whose father constantly reprimanded her for making mistakes. He would berate her for being stupid and clumsy. Talia lived in the belief that she was stupid, and feared making mistakes because of how her father treated her. She could find a lot of evidence to prove how stupid and clumsy she was. She believed that making a mistake was a terrible thing.

As an adult, Talia lived a restricted life by playing it safe and never taking risks. She was constantly in fear of looking stupid or doing something clumsy in front of other people. She couldn't volunteer in her community. She couldn't stand up for herself with a neighbor, even when the neighbor was in the wrong. She believed that her father's perception of her was correct.

Talia started to see her belief as a compilation of thoughts that she revisited many times a day. The thought "I'm stupid" crossed her mind hundreds of times every day, and she believed it. When she started to reflect on the nature of thought, she began to realize that thoughts have no power—unless she believed them. She got curious about why she still believed these thoughts.

Talia also got curious about her father's state of mind back when she was a child. She realized that he was always stressed out and angry. She insightfully saw that if a person's mind is stressed, busy and thinking angry thoughts, the feeling state a person lives in is stressed out and angry. She realized that from this feeling state, people can do inappropriate things and act "dumb"—not necessarily because they want to hurt people, but because they can't fathom that their thinking isn't true. People only mistake poor choices for good ideas from the limited state of mind they are in at the time. Talia saw clearly that her father's behavior had nothing to do with her: it wasn't personal. It was a byproduct of his state of mind.

She started to realize that if her father had had less on his mind, he probably would not have seen her actions as stupid, but as typical childlike accidents. Her thoughts began to lose their grip. She stopped taking her thinking about herself so seriously. When the thought, "I'm so stupid" came to mind, she began to notice it and even laugh at it. In this lighter feeling, Talia saw that she didn't have to live in her past or believe her limiting childhood beliefs about herself anymore. She has even forgiven her father, and is able to view his behavior as an extension of his own state of mind, having nothing to do with her.

Talia has taken a job now that she would have never imagined herself doing before. She doesn't let her old thought habits hold her back from living life to the fullest. She takes risks, makes mistakes and moves on from them, instead of reeling about them in her mind. She has found a sense of freedom and doesn't get uptight when she makes a mistake. She does not identify herself as stupid, although she admits she may sometimes make "stupid" mistakes, as we all do. But when she does, she doesn't take them as personal slights to her character.

I had another client, Amanda, who believed she

wasn't good enough because she thought she was to blame for her parents' divorce. Amanda thought that if she had only behaved better, if she had not acted out, they would not have gotten divorced. The guilt and insecurity she carried around from this false belief affected her own marriage. She always felt she had to give in and be a "good girl" so her husband wouldn't leave her. The fear paralyzed her. She went through her day immersed in all of this thinking from the past. It had nothing to do with her present life, but she kept it alive, unintentionally, via thought.

As Amanda began to discover the nature of thought, she saw that as a little girl she had had no perspective on what was happening. She took everything very personally, and thought the divorce was about her. As a parent, she comprehends that her relationship with her husband has nothing to do with her children and their behavior. She didn't have that perspective then. As her mind settles and she feels her well-being emerge, she can let go of the self-blame and the negative self-talk of not being good enough. Her husband has actually found her newfound security and strength more attractive.

There are many examples of how we bring the past into our present. If we continue to focus on thoughts of blame or resentment whenever we think about someone who hurt us, then our minds rev up. By allowing thoughts such as "They hurt me," "It's not fair," "He took what was rightfully mine," or "I was abused," to be replayed and rehashed in our minds, we cycle through painful memories over and over again. In that cycle, we feel the resentment and bitterness in our bodies as anger, depression or worthlessness. I am not invalidating the pain or the feelings. I am pointing toward how we inadvertently use our minds to torment ourselves. Believe it or not, we don't have to do that anymore. It looks to us as though it's the act of betrayal that is creating our upset right now, but the act of betrayal may have happened 5, 10 or 20 years ago.

Imagine that a person realizes how she is bringing her painful past into the present via the Principle of Thought. She continues to occupy her mind thinking about what was done to her and the hurt and pain it caused her. As she gains insight into what she is unwittingly doing to herself with her mind, she may lose interest in the content of her thoughts, even if she is "right."

I am not saying we should ignore our past or stay in denial about our past. This is an important and misunderstood idea. Denial is never recommended. The Principles point toward how our state of mind determines our experience of life. It does not take away the fact that something really happened. As our state of mind shifts, our perspective about the past shifts as well. When it goes up, the possibility of seeing a bigger picture, gaining perspective or having an original outlook about what happened increases.

This allows for healthy healing of painful past hurts. From a place of health, reflecting on a past hurt—going there in your mind if you need to—may allow you to perceive the situation with perspective. Very often, as our innate resilience emerges, compassion can show up—and maybe even forgiveness. This can be quite healing. This is very different than revisiting your past from a low level of consciousness and creating more revving about the problem. In a busy, resentful and hurt state of mind, a fresh perspective seems impossible. In this state of mind, spinning about old problems or past hurts will be unlikely (to say the least) to lead to healing and peace of mind.

Stated another way, can I be curious about how I can best navigate my relationship to the past? Can I create an opening for something new? From a place of reflection, in a healthy state of mind, I am open to noticing things that weren't visible to me when I was younger, or even yesterday. From that place, I can get an insight that could alter my relationship to my past, as well as my relationship to my thinking about my past.

In a healthy state of mind, I have access to good ideas about how to take care of myself. I have perspective on how having a busy mind or taking something personally may have influenced my experience at the time. I might note that my upset feeling is being created by my thinking, and not the circumstance that I have been blaming my whole life. I might see that I need to ask for forgiveness or give forgiveness. I might realize that I could be alright even if I am still visited by resentment. I might intuit that in order to take care of myself I need to stay away from the person who hurt me.

Who knows what I might see? What we do know

is this: from a place of well-being, resilience surfaces, allowing me to heal my past and live in the present. Can I be open to that possibility, as remote as it might seem?

CHAPTER 6

Tidal Waves

ADDICTIONS

A psychiatrist and well-known Principle-based practitioner, Dr. Pettit, describes addictions from a novel perspective. Imagine somebody who spends 12-14 hours per day thinking in a particular form of thought. For example, imagine someone who's thinking a lot of depressing thoughts: he might be feeling depressed. Someone who's thinking tons of anxious and worrisome thoughts is probably feeling pretty anxious. Someone who's thinking obsessive and compulsive thoughts about their drug of choice might be feeling compelled.

Let's take Tracy, a client who was obsessed with her body, her weight and her food. Here are a few of the thoughts that ran through her head for 12-14 hours a day.

"What am I going to eat or not eat today?" "How am I going to get the food, eat the food and purge the food without anyone noticing?" "Where am I going to hide the food so no one will know I ate it?"

Tracy thought about when to weigh herself, when to reweigh herself, whether to look in the mirror or not look in the mirror, how to turn so her best angle would show in the window as she passed. She thought about whether she should eat breakfast, what was for lunch, what was for dinner. She walked around constantly thinking, "Do they think I'm fat?" And in addition to all that, add all the thinking of guilt and self-deprecation, self-judgment and insecurity she had for not being able to control herself. "I'm a failure," and "There is something wrong with me," were two of her constant companions. Can you picture this?

Any addict who lives in this kind of thinking about their drug of choice is in tremendous turmoil and pain all day. It's exhausting. Believe it or not, the antidote to the pain an addict feels becomes the addiction itself. Whether it's food or narcotics, the drug of choice is taken to alleviate the pain created by all of this thinking. The eating or drug problem becomes the solution to the bigger problem: the hell of thought an addict lives in. From this perspective, if a person can medicate her agitated, uncomfortable feelings, then her addiction becomes her salvation. It's not the problem; it's the solution.

In constricted consciousness, where all urgent feelings stem from, Tracy took her compelled thinking seriously and overate. Could you appreciate how the idea of behavioral therapy to deal with addiction may be two steps too late? The behavior is a result of the uncomfortable feeling, which is a result of the obsessive thinking. If this is true, then the focus should not be on controlling the outcome (whether she binged or purged). It should instead be on directing her toward her inner wisdom, which will guide her to a quieter mind. With perspective, Tracy saw that obsessive and compulsive thoughts are not a problem; they just are. She also understood that they come with a feeling. As soon as she stopped judging the feeling or expecting it to change, she made room for her self-correcting mechanism to do its job.

Acting out with addictive behavior only looked like a good idea to Tracy when she didn't know that her feelings were coming from her thinking rather than what she was thinking *about*. There were many circumstances in her life, including her behavior around food and body issues, that she was blaming for her agitation and frustration. As she learned how her mind worked, she began to see that she was living in the feeling of her thinking. The agitation and frustration came from thought in the moment that she was taking seriously. As Tracy learned to let the urgency pass through her body, her mind naturally began to settle. This happened not because she expended a lot of energy and willpower to control her food, but because she insightfully understood the nature of thought.

Now instead of spending 12-14 hours a day thinking about body, weight and food, Tracy probably spends 10-20 minutes. She doesn't need to eat to alleviate her painful feelings, because most of the obsessive thinking that brought those feelings is no longer on her mind. In her quieter mind, she feels the sweetness and presence of life. In this lighter feeling, it doesn't occur to her to try to escape from her life by eating. Instead, she chooses to embrace her life. Ups and downs don't scare her anymore.

I'll share a personal insight I had when I first learned the Principles, after being in Overeaters Anonymous, a 12-step program, for 12 years. My program didn't solve my "problem" of thinking about food all day. It did however, keep my dysfunctional eating in check. What I realized though, is that I went from obsessing about food and thinking I was fat to obsessing about weighing and measuring my food, making phone calls and getting to meetings. (This doesn't mean this is or should be the insight everyone has, but this is what I saw.)

I still had the "problem" of a busy mind. The only difference was that I was busy working my program rather than busy eating. This was a much healthier solution, but, unbeknownst to me, there was a deeper solution. The deeper solution was learning about the nature of thought and getting curious about the possibility that my thinking was not a problem that needed to be fixed or managed. Seeing my thoughts as temporary, realizing that they would pass and self-correct if I didn't indulge in them, was liberating. I could allow my innate wisdom to bubble up and reveal my health. As it did, it occurred to me that I didn't need to continue believing that I had a problem, that I would never be normal. From a quieter mind, I didn't perceive a problem.

Today, I believe that we all have access to our innate health. It's a gift to live from a place of gratitude. I am grateful that all the obsessive, compulsive thinking about food and body is no longer a part of my life. I am not going to pretend it happened overnight for me. However, I had a client, Sydney, who had been anorexic for most of her life. After attending a seminar and a private session she had an epiphany and said, "Oh my gosh, I don't have an eating disorder. It was all my thinking."

There are many stories of an insight blowing someone's addictive thinking out of the water. Even without one mind-blowing insight, through slow and steady insights, I found my way back to my health. Insightful thought guided me to see that my relationship to food, dieting and exercising were all thought-created. I learned that:

☞ I didn't have to take all of my thinking seriously.

☞ Thought, even repetitive thought, is not a problem.

☞ I don't have to believe the judgmental thoughts I have about myself for having obsessive thinking or acting out on it.

☞ I don't have to beat myself up for having any kind of thinking because I am not my thinking.

☞ I can trust that my wisdom will guide me to take care of myself.

☞ Regardless of my state of mind, I am doing the best I can given the thinking I am having in the moment.

Today I'm OK with my humanity. Food, and thought about food, is a non-issue in my life, thank God. Imagine if that were possible with any kind of compulsive thinking.

PART III

SURFING IN ACTION

Life-Changing Insights

CHAPTER 1

Don't Make Waves

THE THOUGHT-FEELING CONTINUUM

A ll thought falls somewhere on the thought-feeling continuum. Regardless of where you fall, every person has the capacity for insight. Everyone can benefit from understanding the human condition. We all have the ability to reveal more of our innate health than we are presently experiencing.

The continuum is a metaphor for how we experience thought. The more repetitive a certain thought is, the more gripped we are by it. The more gripped we are by our thinking, the more intense and compelling our feeling state becomes. In this type of feeling state, anyone might behave in ways that can be interpreted as impulsive, obsessive or destructive. Nevertheless, underneath it all, every human being is innately healthy. Take a look at the graph below of the thought-feeling continuum. Keep in mind that the distinction between where one category ends and another begins may be a bit arbitrary.

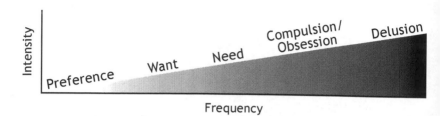

The only difference between someone on the left end of the spectrum (preference or want) and someone on the right end of the spectrum (obsession or delusion) is the frequency and intensity with which thought visits them. The intensity of feeling in their body is directly proportionate to the frequency of thought.

BOARDWALK CONCESSIONS

Imagine we are at the beach and I ask you, "Would you like ice cream? Which do you prefer, chocolate or vanilla?" Let's say you prefer chocolate (that's what I prefer). Then I say, "Oops, they are out of chocolate. They only have vanilla." You may decide to have vanilla instead, or you may just skip the ice cream. It's not a big deal. You won't be really upset about it. It would have been a nice treat in the heat, but you can move on easily. At the level of preference, the frequency and the intensity of the thought of chocolate ice cream is basically nonexistent. You probably weren't thinking about it before I asked you. If you wanted some once I offered, you probably won't continue to think about it now that it's not available.

What if I ask, "Would you like ice cream?" and you want it? You might continue to think about the ice cream even after I tell you they don't have chocolate. You might feel a little disappointed that you didn't get ice cream. What a tease! At the level of want, the frequency and the intensity of the thought of ice cream can come and go. Chances are you will move on with your day. It would have been nice, but oh well.

If I ask you, "Would you like ice cream?" and you need ice cream, but then I say, "Oops, sorry, they are out of ice cream," what is your reaction going to be? If you need ice cream, you're not going to take this one sitting down. At the level of need, the frequency and the intensity of the thought of ice cream is higher. The thoughts will be stronger and you are going to feel a lack in your body if you don't get the ice cream. You might not be able to enjoy lying on the beach anymore without thinking about ice cream. The thought of ice cream is going to linger and you may not be able to override it. You may not accept that they don't have ice cream, and you might decide you'll look for another ice cream shop on the boardwalk.

Now what if you don't just need the ice cream, but you begin to obsess over the ice cream? The craving and urge (another word for a thought that feels intensely strong) takes over your mind. You are compelled to think about the ice cream non-stop as soon as I mention the word "ice cream." At the level of compulsion/obsession, the frequency and the intensity of the thoughts about ice cream will feel unbearable. The feeling in your body of having to eat ice cream in order to function will overtake you. Lying on the beach only thinking about ice cream won't seem like an option. The need to walk on the boardwalk until you find ice cream will compel you. You might make an excuse to go to the bathroom just to look now. You may even drive to a 7-11 if you can't find an ice cream vendor on the boardwalk, buy a pint and eat it in the parking lot. You will not be able to think about anything else until the craving is met. Your body will not alleviate your agitation until the ice cream is eaten.

Imagine I ask, "Would you like ice cream?" Then I realize I don't have any and apologize. But you believe strongly that I do have ice cream. You even think I am hiding it from you because a voice told you that I locked it up just so you can't have any. At the level of delusion, the frequency and the intensity of the thoughts around ice cream are so strong that there is no differentiation between reality and fantasy. For a person at the level of delusion, thoughts are not just their perception, but they seem so real that a person can feel, taste, smell or hear them. That person's reality is that they are really hearing voices. They really believe someone is out to get them.

You can see by looking at the thought-feeling continuum how your experience of not having ice cream changes depending on the frequency and intensity of the thinking you are having in the moment. As our relationship to our thinking shifts, wants, needs and obsessions, even delusions, can lose their grip. We begin to lose interest in the content of what we are wanting, needing or obsessing about.

LOW TIDE

I want to shine a light on how our experience of the question "Would you like ice cream?" is coming from within us, depending on the frequency and intensity of the thoughts we have about it. Getting a glimpse of this is extremely helpful. How many of us believe the thoughts we have about what we need? We don't realize that we are inadvertently creating our own pain, our own feeling of lack, that has nothing to do with whether or not our "needs" are being met.

I had a client, Naomi, who believed she needed her husband, Jeff, to be emotionally available. From Naomi's perspective, he wasn't. She wanted to leave him. I am not sharing my opinion about whether this was a real need of hers or not. What I tried to highlight for Naomi was that she was feeling her own thinking more than she was feeling the emotional availability of her husband.

At the level of need, the frequency and the intensity of constantly thinking "My husband isn't emotionally available!" does not bode well for the marriage. We got curious about the possibility of relating to this as a preference. The aim was not for Naomi to convince herself that she didn't need emotional availability from Jeff, or for her to reframe her feelings. Rather, it was a way to create an opening for an insight, a way for her to see that she was creating her own frustration via thought. If Naomi continued to focus on what she already "knew" about Jeff (that he was not emotionally available), then she would limit her chance to see something else.

Meaning, Naomi had an expectation of what a husband would be like and if she was willing to let go of that, maybe something new would occur to her. What if it would have been a nice thing for him to listen to her until the cows came home, but it wasn't a deal-breaker if he couldn't? I invited her to reconsider the "truth" that her thoughts had her believing.

Once she let go of her expectation that she "needed" this from him, the intensity of her feeling of lack diminished. Naomi started to notice Jeff's other qualities. He was responsible and kind, he paid the bills and he helped with the kids. Naomi may still have moments where she chooses to indulge in her this-is-what-I-need thinking, but now she understands how it destroys her warm feelings for her husband when she does. Jeff really does love her, but he shows it in a different way than she expected. Actually, in time he became more emotionally available. I still don't know if his behavior changed or her perception of his behavior changed, but I'm pleased to report that they are happily married today. Often, as we internally shift by quieting down, we act out less against others. Those around us then tend to settle down as well.

SLEEPING ON DECK

Understanding the thought-feeling continuum is so helpful in many areas of life. One area where I find this discovery to be particularly helpful is sleep. Many people struggle with the issue of sleep. Have you ever spent time tossing and turning, getting more and more frazzled that you can't fall asleep or can't fall back asleep? How often do we lie there thinking, "This is such a problem! I need to sleep. I can't function if I don't get enough sleep. I am so sleep deprived, I may kill someone. This is no joke. Please, help me fall asleep." Yet the tossing and turning continues as we lie there ruminating, unable to fall asleep. We play over the day's events, replaying conversations that we had or need to have, planning all our to-dos...our minds just don't want to stop for a minute to let us rest.

When we obsess about falling asleep, or even when we focus on how much we need to fall asleep, sleep tends to elude us. The "is-ness" in the moment is that we are lying in our bed awake. Then we overlay what is with all of our thinking about it and wonder why we can't fall asleep. We have the thought, "I won't be able to function if I don't fall asleep," and we believe this is "the truth" rather than a thought passing through our minds. When we take our thinking about "the truth" seriously by focusing on it, we innocently bring on more of those thoughts and anxious feelings. Then we wonder why we can't fall asleep.

What if I was willing to experiment with the thought-feeling continuum? If my mind quieted down and I went from obsessing about falling asleep to wanting to fall asleep, or from needing to sleep to preferring to sleep, what would happen? What if not falling asleep wasn't a problem? "It would be nice to fall asleep, but I'm OK even if I don't. I can just lay here relaxing. I can read a book or watch something."

Are you being attacked by thoughts right now at the mere suggestion that you consider this idea? Are you thinking: "What do you mean? I do need to fall asleep. I have a family, I have a job; I have to function! What are you talking about? It's not a preference like ice cream. I could live without ice cream for the rest of my life. I can't live without sleep!"

I'm only inviting you to wonder about your attachment to sleep. (Mind you, sleep is only the content of this example. You can fill in the blank with any example that you find yourself obsessing over. Some other common examples include the need to understand, the need for clarity and the need to control your children's choices.) As the frequency of our thoughts lessens, so does the intensity of our feelings. Are we willing to get out of our own way and be open to an unconventional relationship to sleep?

HANG LOOSE

Do we prefer to feel good, want to feel good, need to feel good, or obsess about how to feel good? Our beliefs about feeling good (or about not feeling bad) directly create our experience. There seems to be a focus on numbing out these days. Our society is obsessed with the idea that it's a problem to feel bad. We don't even know how to feel; we just know we are afraid to feel because it might be uncomfortable.

If we allowed ourselves to feel uncomfortable, maybe we would be totally fine. Most of our discomfort comes from the fearful thinking we have about feeling bad, anxious or depressed. It's this added thought, which we don't even see as thought, that weighs us down. We are left with a pile of thought in our heads the height of the Empire State Building, and then we wonder why we feel so uncomfortable in our own skin. If we dropped the added fear, we would actually be fine feeling a little worry, sadness or even anxiety, because feelings aren't a problem.

What if our goal wasn't to feel good? What if feeling bad wasn't a problem? What if uncomfortable feelings were just an indication of thought passing through our minds? Since we are feeling our thinking all of the time, there is no reason to fear any feeling, or any thought for that matter. True, our thinking will look and feel real in a low state of mind, but it can't hurt us. No thought or feeling can hurt us unless we fail to notice it as thought and then act on it.

Some people question the detachment that seems to be implied here. I can hear you saying, "I mean, if nothing is ever a problem, if I never wanted or needed anything, then life would be emotionless. I like my intensity. I'm passionate about what I want and what I believe. I don't want to be detached." Good for you! I am also intense and passionate about life. Intensity and passion are not what we are trying to detach from. Psychological freedom comes when we detach from *opinions* and *beliefs* we hold as true, not because we choose to believe them, but out of habit.

We detach from our emotion about our personal thinking, not our emotion about life. We disengage from our virtual reality in order to engage in actual reality. When we do this, we are better able to access our emotional well-being and to feel present more of the time. It's true, we end up detaching from certain feelings in the process. But we do this as a means to the end of ultimately increasing our free choice. The detachment is in no way meant to be an excuse to deny our feelings.

I had a client, Mia, who was suicidal. As she learned about the Principles, she began to believe that she was innately healthy, regardless of her suicidal thoughts. At some point, it became apparent that she was using what she had learned about detachment to stay in denial about the abuse she had experienced as a child. If she didn't think, she wouldn't feel. But we were not meant to be emotionless beings. We are meant to be able to feel, whether it is pain, fear and disappointment, or gratitude, clarity and love. Once Mia gave herself permission to feel, she began to heal.

There's a whole range of emotion to feel because there is a whole range of thought to have. The goal is not to take away the human experience of having emotions. We want to be able to feel anything, but we also want to know when we are feeling reality versus feeling the illusions we make up about reality. Giving ourselves permission to feel the gamut of emotions, to feel life to the fullest, is a gift. We can feel excited, lonely, agitated, grateful—it's all fine because it's coming from thought flowing through the system. We don't have to judge an experience as bad just because it's uncomfortable. We don't have to "need" to feel good. We could feel how we feel and not make it mean anything about ourselves.

A healthy detachment from our personal thoughts allows us to process painful experiences while being connected to our wisdom and the Source of that wisdom. This connection gives us clarity about what is and is not necessary to feel in order to move on to a place of health and healing.

The thinking-feeling connection is so immediate. It is like flicking on the light switch and the light coming on: it happens instantaneously. But have you ever used low energy light bulbs? When you switch them on for the first time in the morning, they actually take a few seconds to slowly brighten. To me, learning about the nature of thought gives me that slight, momentary pause. It's a wedge that creates enough of an opening between me and my thinking for a pause to occur.

In that moment, if I can see thought as separate from myself, I have free choice. I can strengthen that muscle, that will to listen for insight. As I get better at it, I become aware of when detaching from my beliefs and opinions could be helpful. I can feel whatever happens (whether I believe it was decreed by God, or not) without making it worse with my added habitual thinking. Is there any feeling I need to be afraid of having? In a connected, healthy place, I can feel pain, discomfort and sadness fully, and not be afraid of any of it. However, in a disconnected, unhealthy place, the pain, discomfort and sadness can take on a life of its own. Can I grasp the difference?

CHANNEL SURFING

What is boredom? Boredom is just a symptom of an overactive mind. Does this sound counterintuitive to you? Most people think boredom comes because they have nothing to do and nothing on their minds. Really, what's happening is that our minds are used to being revved up. We have become accustomed to our minds moving fast. When there isn't something happening and we slow down even a little bit, we find ourselves uncomfortable in that space. We then label that feeling as boredom.

If I prefer not to be bored, but I have nothing to

do in this moment, I'll wait for it to pass and it won't really be such a big deal. But if being bored is a problem and I need to be doing something, my mind will be revving about what to do. I've even seen people obsessively resist boredom, and go to any lengths to keep themselves from feeling bored

If the thought "I'm bored" crosses my mind, it will most likely look true. However, it only becomes a problem when I think being bored is a problem. If I remember that thought is ever-flowing, I will realize that I can't stay bored for very long. Even if I could, so what?

My kids know that whenever they come to me and say that they are bored, I either say, "Good!" or "Let's see how long you can stay bored." Although they can't stand my answer, they do know that being bored is not a problem, a bad thing or something I feel responsible to do anything about. As their minds settle down from thinking of boredom as a problem, they eventually have an idea and find something to do. Before they know it, they forget that they were ever bored.

Can I be open to the possibility that my wants and needs may be thought-created rather than circumstance-driven? My experience of them can change as my relationship to my wants and needs shifts. Am I willing to experiment with loosening my grip on what I believe I need?

CHAPTER 2

We're All in the Same Boat

SEEING THE PSYCHOLOGICAL INNOCENCE IN OTHERS

My intention is to awaken an awareness that our experience of life is coming from within us, from our thinking moment to moment, and not from our external circumstances. So too, all of the people in our lives are operating from the same Principles. When we become aware of different states of mind that visit humanity, it helps us to navigate our relationships with others. Just as there is freedom in not taking myself so seriously, there is a freedom that comes from not taking everyone else's speech and actions so personally. What people say and do is always an indicator of their state of mind. What if I were listening for another person's state of mind, rather than getting caught up in what they are actually saying or doing?

I had a client, Mindy, who had a daughter, Ilana. Ilana's rebellious behavior was getting her in a lot of trouble. She had been thrown out of her second school, and Mindy brought her to me as a last resort, hoping that I could help her to stop acting out. As I talked to Mindy about the nature of thought, she struggled with understanding how this learning was going to change Ilana's problematic behavior. It was hard for her not to judge Ilana and her actions. The behaviors Ilana was displaying were so over-the-top, from Mindy's perspective, that she couldn't find it within herself to judge her favorably.

Mindy had no visibility to the role that thought was playing in her experience of her daughter. All she could see was that Ilana's behaviors appeared real to her. Ilana really was abusive, nasty and bullying. Mindy wasn't making it up, and she wasn't crazy. Everyone around Ilana was fed up.

At this point, Mindy knew that she didn't like the feeling in her body when she was filled with rage at her daughter. She didn't like yelling like a lunatic, and she knew it wasn't good for her other children to see her like that. She got a glimpse of the fact that her feelings were coming from her thinking, rather than being triggered by her circumstances, in other areas of her life. For example, she saw at work that her insecure thinking affected her productivity. She saw that her judgmental attitude with her sister created unnecessary tension in the family. She also saw that when she dropped it, family gatherings were much nicer for her. Nonetheless, she hadn't had any insights regarding her daughter, yet.

As Mindy experimented, she noticed that when she was in a better state of mind, she wasn't so quick to yell. Then one day, in the midst of a meltdown, all of the sudden—WHAM!—it occurred to her: "Ilana also must not like the feeling in her body when she is explosive and acting abusively to her siblings or intimidating me. I bet if she were in a better state of mind, she wouldn't say and do such hurtful things to us."

Mindy honestly saw that Ilana was simply lost in her thinking and she didn't know it...yet. We all get lost in our thinking and wish we didn't. Ilana had no visibility to that fact that her anger was coming from her thinking. She thought it was coming from her siblings and her parents. If she knew better, she wouldn't have acted that way. This insight was a game changer for Mindy.

Mindy went on to describe how, for the first time ever, a huge wave of compassion came over her. She saw her daughter's pain rather than her defiance. She didn't do anything to make it happen. She wasn't working on controlling her temper at the time. She just experienced a flash of insight which beamed her up to the penthouse, and as the elevator doors opened, compassion was there. It was so obvious. It enveloped her whole being.

If someone had given her good advice about how to feel compassion for her daughter, it wouldn't have been successful. You can't fake a compassionate feeling. If Ilana had gotten a whiff of any lingering annoyance or judgment on Mindy's part, the connection would have been lost. The rapport would have been dead in the water. She couldn't have forced herself to feel compassion even if she wanted to. With insight, you don't have to act as if you feel compassion—you truly feel it.

In a nicer feeling, when two Divine souls come together, love, compassion and forgiveness is what naturally appears. It doesn't take much effort to let go of personal thinking when we see the truth of who another person is. Seeing this truth is a gift from the Divine Himself. I can try all I want to force myself to see it or to reframe my personal thinking, but it won't have the same impact and it will take a lot of effort.

When the gift of seeing the innocence in another human being is granted, you will know it by the feeling that arises within you. Mindy's whole relationship to her thinking about her daughter shifted. The nature of their relationship did a complete 180-degree turnabout starting with that initial shift in perspective. Although this shift was not used as a technique in order to change Ilana's behavior, Mindy was pleasantly surprised to see that, in time, her daughter's behavior improved. The warm feeling of understanding between them lent itself to better interactions, mutual respect and an overall better relationship, which filtered down to the other siblings.

This is the power of insightfully seeing the humanity in others. We are all doing the best we can given the thinking we are having at the time. It's nothing personal; it's just part of the human condition. We all get lost. We don't have to beat ourselves up for getting lost, and we don't have to beat others up either (with words or in our minds). We can see innocence in our own humanity as well as in the humanity of others.

You may be thinking, "That sounds like a nice idea in theory, but people aren't really all that innocent, and some do really nasty things. They hurt intentionally, disrespect relentlessly and destroy relationships deliberately. How can you say they are innocent? These are behaviors that have a real impact. There is real hurt being inflicted. How could I pretend that's not happening? Do I have to let go of the hurt and forgive? Am I supposed to be an angel?"

Psychological innocence does not imply lack of responsibility. A person who acts out from a compulsive and urgent feeling is completely responsible for the consequences of his actions and should be held accountable. However, his free choice may have been limited. His actions are a reflection of *his* state of mind, not a reflection of *me* personally. I don't have to continue to see myself as a victim.

We are human beings having a human experience. I am only directing our attention to where our experience of life comes from in the moment. I am not suggesting how to use your mind once you understand how your mind works. Just know that whatever is on your mind (hurt, resentment, anger) is what you feel in the moment. When you look to blame other people for your feelings, you are innocently living in the misunderstanding of where your feelings are coming from in the first place.

I had another client, Adina, who had been physically abused by her mother throughout her childhood. As she learned about the nature of thought, she felt her innate health emerge (something she didn't believe she even had). She became more and more aware of the anxious feeling in her body whenever the caller ID showed her mother was calling. That feeling began to tip her off to when she was indulging in low-quality thinking about her mother. As her mind settled and she had less thinking about her mother, her feeling state around her mother shifted.

At some point Adina was touched by the idea that all human beings are psychologically innocent and would never hurt someone when in a healthy state of mind. Adina deeply saw her mother's suffering and how the abusive behavior was more about her mother's state of mind than about her personally. In a place of security, no one does things to hurt themselves or others. Hurt only happens when someone unsuspectingly believes their low-quality thinking to be true. Adina speaks publicly now about how she has completely forgiven her mother and actually has a pleasant relationship with her today. She also doesn't see value in living in the past when she has a blessed life today. Although this example may sound dramatic, is it possible for us to see the psychological innocence in ourselves and others, too?

CHAPTER 3

Still Waters Run Deep

BUSY MIND VS. QUIET MIND

Have you ever gone to a conference where there are five or six amazing speakers presenting at the same time? You can't even decide which one to go to, right? I was at one such conference with my friend, Susie, and she picked one of the classes from the schedule. The whole time she sat there thinking (and saying to me under her breath), "I should have gone to the other one. I knew I should have gone to the other one."

Now if Susie is busy thinking about being somewhere else, is she present in the room with the actual speaker? We are either in our heads or we are in our lives. If Susie's head is spinning—judging the presenter, blaming herself for making a bad choice, expecting to learn something specific—is she able to hear anything being presented? From her perspective, the speaker is controlling her experience. She's judging whether or not he is doing a good job entertaining her, teaching her or making her feel good. It really looks to Susie as if the reason she isn't enjoying herself at the lecture is because she picked the wrong speaker.

What do you think happened when someone asked her, "Susie, how was the lecture?" She replied, "He wasn't such a great speaker and the topic was a bit boring. I knew the other presenter would have been a better choice." She believed she was sharing "the truth," not just her perspective.

If Susie understood that her experience of that speaker came from within her, she probably would not have walked out and said something disparaging about him. If she had been gifted to notice that she was feeling her thinking, not her circumstances, she may have realized, "Wait a minute. If I was sitting in this class feeling agitated, the quality of my thinking must have been low. Maybe I was busy judging and evaluating rather than being present. I was in my head instead of in the room with the speaker. My mind was filled with static. Maybe I shouldn't give my opinion about the class until my mind settles down."

There are so many examples of static that keeps our minds busy. How often do we have a thought that we want to share with someone when they haven't finished speaking yet? We are afraid that we are going to forget it, so we focus on it, not realizing that we have stopped listening. How many of us have felt frustrated by a co-worker asking for advice? She is venting, and all we can think about is how she is wasting our time. How many of us have ever driven somewhere when our minds were everywhere but on the road? We are shocked when we arrive at our destinations because we can't recall the ride. Or we are playing with our kids and our minds are distracted with everything else we would rather be doing. Or we are praying, and somehow we find ourselves at the end of our prayer and realize we weren't paying attention to the words because we were interested in the lists we were making in our heads.

Any habit of thought, regardless of the flavor, acts as static. If we pay attention to it, we will become busier in our minds because of it. Since a busy mind comes with a feeling, we can use this feeling as a barometer to let us know when we are lost. Just as we can feel it, others around us can also feel it. All children know whether an adult is listening to them or pretending to listen because their mind is someplace else.

Our minds are like a ceiling fan. My son once decided to do an experiment and see if he could get a broom handle through the blades. On high speed, he almost broke the fan. On low speed, he was actually able to get it through. On high speed, the blades spin so fast that it looks like one big blade and it feels as if nothing can get through: neither a new thought nor an insight. On low speed, each individual blade is distinct as it spins around, and there is space for original ideas to come in.

I didn't realize my mind was on the high setting most of the day because the feeling of urgency was familiar to me. It never occurred to me there might be another way to live until I started to learn about how we create the experience of urgency via thought. I had never considered the idea that time is a reflection of our state of mind rather than a reality we are locked into. Someone told me a joke once: how long does a minute take? It depends on which side of the bathroom door you are on. Although that may be a bit crass, it makes the point. In an urgent, rushed, it's-gotta-be-now feeling, a minute feels like forever. In a calm, slower place, a minute is a minute. The flip side is also true. Sometimes in a mad rush, a minute is never enough time, while in a place of calm, a minute can be very full. It's not time per se, but my relationship to time that creates my urgency or peace of mind.

As my mind went from boiling to simmering, I started to have thoughts such as, "Maybe all that rushing around isn't so productive," and "Maybe I'm not getting as much done as I think I'm getting done." Instead of overriding these thoughts, as I had done in the past, I was willing to listen to them. Having less on my mind eventually became comfortable, even something I appreciated and valued. In the wake of these insights, I started choosing to slow down and rush less. As a result, a different feeling, an internal sense of calm, started to visit me more often. I was pleasantly surprised to see that I was actually more productive doing what needed to be done from this calm feeling state.

I started to become a connoisseur of my feeling state. I began to value the insight when I noticed I was compelled. I lost interest in the belief that running around, multi-tasking and being busy was always a valuable use of my time. I experimented with allowing myself to have quiet time and learned what it felt like. I began using this feeling state as a guide to know whether I was present and accessing my wisdom or not. I realized that the key to approaching all of my problems is my state of mind. Although I can't control my state of mind or the thoughts that visit me, experiencing a sense of urgency informs me to wait it out until my state of mind shifts. In a quieter mind, I experience being present in my life. Presence also comes with a feeling.

In a quieter mind, we experience insights and wisdom flowing through us. Many of us get duped into thinking that our circumstances created the insight or good feeling. For instance, I've had clients tell me how their 12-step program changed everything. Others assure me that a certain type of therapy, a transformative seminar they attended or a book they read changed their thinking or perspective. Although the transformation may have happened while "doing" any one of these things, the Principles are pointing toward the determining factor in all of these situations. When we have less on our minds, we feel better. When our state of mind shifts, we gain perspective.

When we attend a program, therapy or seminar, or even when we read a book, if we give ourselves permission (consciously or unconsciously) to unwind and listen, we will feel differently than when we started. In the process, our minds begin to settle and our internal self-correcting mechanism begins to work. We listen more deeply, gain insights and feel present. I am not knocking any program that is here to help. I am suggesting that the shifts come from within you, not from the program.

I had a client, Debbie, who started thinking that learning about the Principles of Innate Health was creating her better feeling. I directed her right back to where her experience was truly coming from—her state of mind in the moment. Although it appeared to her that she needed to come to my office or listen to a class online in order to quiet down, the external "thing" did not cause her to quiet down. There may have been a correlation, but it was not cause and effect. There were times when she remained spinning even after listening to an online class.

Debbie once summed it up nicely. She said, "I'd never spent time with someone who is sincerely present before meeting you. At first it was uncomfortable, especially when there was silence. But then I realized my discomfort was a result of being in touch with my own busy mind. As my mind settled down, I began to feel much better." She intuitively understood that in the space of a soul to soul connection, something happens. An opportunity is created where we give ourselves permission to let our minds settle and to experience our innate health. Stepping into that space can be like a contact high. It's palpable and contagious, but it's an internal job. Can we give ourselves permission to settle down? Can we use our feeling state to indicate the speed of our minds?

CHAPTER 4

Surf's Up

TAKING MYSELF LESS SERIOUSLY

I had no idea that a belief was just thought in another form. I thought my beliefs were true, just like I believed my thoughts were true. Our lives seem to be made up of beliefs by which we then define ourselves. Some beliefs we actually thought out and chose, while others we just took on because everyone around us believed them. Regardless of why we believe what we do, beliefs are already formed thoughts that come with a feeling.

I was acutely aware of a familiar feeling: one of intensity, heaviness and seriousness. It felt real to me that life was meant to be taken seriously. I thought, "I have a purpose: a mission that only I can fulfill. I am going to be accountable for how I use my time and whether or not I maximize my potential." Although the content of my beliefs may even be true, the content is not the most important factor in determining whether to focus upon, trust or value my beliefs. Rather, the determining factor is where I am in the elevator when I am focusing upon, trusting or valuing my beliefs. Reflecting on my beliefs in the penthouse has one feeling to it, while brooding on my beliefs in the basement has another feeling to it.

In a higher state of consciousness, I can reflect on what I need to do in order to use my time wisely and maximize my potential. However, more often than not, I found myself in a low level of consciousness while ruminating about how I was not doing enough, not being enough, or wasting too much time. I took every decision and action very seriously while in this state of mind. It should be no shock that I walked around feeling uptight, high-strung and stressed out. I'm sure I was fun to be around in that state...not!

The craziest part is that in this state of mind, the cards were stacked against me. What I needed most was wisdom to guide me, yet I was unintentionally focusing on the content of my thinking from the basement. I believed there was value in intensely analyzing everything in order to figure out the important things in life.

I also believed there was value in my opinions and perceptions of other people. Beliefs such as: "People who don't take life and their thinking seriously are irresponsible," or "People who are laid-back are slackers," or "People who aren't intense are superficial." Imagine being someone in my life on the other end of my judgments!

I had no idea that my thinking wasn't true, that my judgment wasn't right. I had no clue that all my beliefs about intensity and the seriousness of life were holding me back from reaching my goals rather than motivating me to reach them. I wasn't aware that these kinds of beliefs were keeping me from experiencing life with pleasure, grace and compassion. I began to see that taking life seriously, as well as taking everything personally, were misguided beliefs that I had because of the fact that I was in the basement.

If my husband came home with a new idea for a program, I would explain why it wouldn't work. I thought I was being practical, a realist, when really all I could think about was how this new program was going to affect *me*. What was he going to expect *me* to do to make this idea happen? This is a perfect example of how my listening was tainted by staying in what I know ("This is going to affect me."), expectations ("He expects me to make this happen."), and judgment ("Not another new idea."). Doesn't that sound like a busy mind to you?

Not only was I taking my thinking seriously about my husband, other people and life, but I was taking my thinking about myself seriously. This can create a tremendous amount of pain when the content is self-deprecating and negative. As I was feeling guilty and selfish for not wanting to help my husband, it hit me one day: "Wait a minute...I'm not selfish; I'm just having a self-conscious thought storm. I'm drinking the poison and hoping to be cured."

With awareness we can stop the engagement, regardless of how true it looks. We can wait for the intensity to pass. The feeling state of intensity is a barometer that lets me know that the quality of my thinking is low. Once I became aware of what I was unintentionally doing to myself with my own self-conscious thinking, I began to lose interest in the content. I became an objective observer to my thoughts rather than being one with them. It was as if I was able to watch my thoughts like the breaking news ticker at the bottom of the TV news screen. I naturally began to take my thinking less seriously, including the part where I made everything about me.

I was able to hear my husband say, "We are out of milk," and respond, "OK, I'll try to get more today," instead of personalizing his comment and thinking it was a statement about my incompetence. I was able to be open to his latest initiative, to see if he requested my involvement, and then decide whether I was able to help. I was able to notice the habitual thought of "I'm stupid," and step back from it. That thought was not me. I could watch it flow down the stream.

It started occurring to me to let my thought storms flow down the stream and wait for a quieter mind. In the space of a quieter mind, reflecting on my life's purpose and how I wanted to use my time seemed reasonable. In a lighter feeling, my wisdom guided me. Sometimes the guidance was to consult a friend, professional or rabbi. Other times, it was to wait for a nicer feeling to emerge.

It is liberating to have choice about lightening up and taking ourselves and our thinking less seriously. We don't have to believe our thoughts are true just because we think them. Are we willing to get curious about the truth of our negative self-talk? Are we willing to experiment with letting an insecure thought storm pass, while allowing a force beyond ourselves to heal our thinking?

CHAPTER 5

Bridge Over Troubled Water

NAVIGATING LIFE'S UPS AND DOWNS WITH GRACE

I n summary, the implications of looking out at life with a different pair of glasses are profound. Once I intuit that my experience is coming from within me, all of that excess energy spent trying to control, manipulate or blame my environment or the people in my life seems like a waste of time. How much time could we spend debating the nature vs. nurture argument, the importance of reliving the past, the reasons we are victims in life, or our self-righteous perspective? Why do we debate? To be right? Does that affect our well-being or sense of inner peace?

So much dialogue falls away when we have the clarity that thought and consciousness determine how we feel. It is clear to me that my sense of security, satisfaction and contentment are not coming from my external environment. They come when I have an internal shift in my relationship to my thinking about these things.

We are all doing the best we can given our thinking and level of consciousness in the moment. The goal here is not to control, change or manage our thinking in order to bring about more clarity or insightful thoughts. By definition, we cannot produce an insight via our personal thinking. Nevertheless, insight is always available.

Some may question, "How is it possible for insight to *always* be available?" An analogy could be made to the Internet, where information is always available to us. We just have to type something in and answers appear. Whether we are searching for something or not...the answers are always there. We are innately healthy, regardless of the thinking we are having at the time. As our attention is diverted from our health, we may not feel it. Trusting that Thought and Consciousness are being guided by the Divine power of Mind allows me to ride the wave of my thinking without too much concern for its content.

There are many implications of allowing the system to work. Here are just a few:

↝ We don't have to fixate on any one thought, or on any content that is coming through our minds at any given moment.

↝ We know where to orient for a fresh, new thought.

↝ We know what to respect and what to value, as well as what not to respect nor value.

☞ We listen to our feeling state as a barometer for the quality of our thinking in the moment.

What is so practical about this? Since my body is a biofeedback machine, it will always tell me where I am on the spectrum. When my mind gets busy and the feeling in my body is one of urgency, this is valuable information that can guide me. I don't want to give the content a lot of attention. I don't want to respect my opinions, perceptions and conclusions or value my ideas in this space. My feeling state tells me whether I am off track and if I should wait for the system to "recalculate."

However, when my mind settles and the compelling feeling is replaced with inner peace, my consciousness goes up. The thought that shows up for me in this space is something I want to reflect upon, respect and value. From this state of mind, I look to have the conversations that need to be had. This is the space where I want to talk to my child about the mistake he made, answer a heated email from a customer, or discuss the bills with my husband.

The more we see the psychological innocence in ourselves and others, the more flexible and fluid our experience of life becomes. The understanding alone serves life up to us in a nicer feeling state. If you don't see this possibility yet, hang in there. It is available for all human beings. The moment we notice that we are living in the misunderstanding of where our experience is coming from, we get a hit of, "Oh yeah, I'm experiencing my thinking." This spark alters my experience without my having to work at making that happen.

As a participant in one of my Professional Development courses said, "If I have clarity that life is like a roller coaster rather than a runaway train, I can enjoy the ride." Understanding the human condition is the most practical, hands-on way to navigate the roller coaster ride of life. When we know how it works, the eeriness of the unknown doesn't spook us.

My nephew had to get his tonsils out when he was five years old. My sister-in-law decided that if he understood the procedure, it would help with his anxiety. She took him to the hospital the day before and explained it to him. "This is the room where we will wait for them to call us. This is the room where you will change your clothes and get in a gown. This is the room where they will take out your tonsils. This is the room where you will recover and feel some pain, but afterwards in that room they will give you yummy ice cream and treats." It worked like a charm. He knew he could endure the pain because the next room had treats waiting for him.

So too, if we understand the different levels of consciousness and what happens when we are in our thinking and feeling states, we don't have to be spooked. We just know: in this room, we feel really bad because all the nasty, scary thoughts look and feel real. We may be plagued with depression, anxiety, hopelessness, fear or insecurity, but at some point we will move to another room. In that room, we have a little more perspective and feel a little better. In that room, where all the yummy treats are, we will feel calm, peaceful, grateful, wise, clear and whole.

If I understand the nature of thought, then I trust that thought is ever-flowing and at some point, new thought will flow in. My state of mind will change, my level of consciousness will rise, and I will have more perspective on life. Navigation means we are doing the best we can, allowing for our internal GPS to recalculate when necessary. If I try to have an interaction with my boss or my spouse, and I realize my state of mind just dropped twenty stories, it might be a good idea to push off the conversation if I can. If I can't, I'll do the best I can given my state of mind and hope for the best—while having an inkling that my perception may be jaded (even though I feel 100% convinced that I am right). This inkling allows me to navigate in what I have coined "damage control" mode.

Damage control mode is where we try to do as little damage as possible when placed in a situation where we have to act while our state of mind is compromised. That inkling of skewed perception is our consciousness in action. When we are gifted to listen to it, we are grateful that the damage is minimal, and we wait for our internal psychological immune system to reset itself. When it does, we have the wisdom we need to clean up any mess we may have made in the process of being human.

I have had clients whose habit is a spinning mind, worry about what will happen when they are finally in a good mood. Unintentionally, they pay attention to their habit by focusing on thoughts like, "It's not going to last," or, "Before I turn around, the rug will be pulled out from under me," or, "I don't deserve to feel this good." I remind them that if a thought like that passes through their mind, it will look and feel real and become their experience. It should be no surprise, then, when they don't experience a good mood.

Before we even have a chance to revel in the good feeling, we inadvertently knock ourselves out of the ball game with thought. Some of us don't allow ourselves to ride the wave when we're high because we don't see our habitual thinking as thought in the moment. We get duped into believing it's the truth. When we are gifted to notice that these are just thoughts, with no basis in reality, the habit loses its grip, and we start experiencing nicer moments in a quieter mind. When this happens, we are visited by presence and connection. The more we feel it, the more familiar it becomes and the easier it is to allow ourselves to be there. We can be grateful and ride the wave while it's here. I have personally found that being grateful for these moments seems to bring them on more frequently. Let's enjoy the feeling while we're in it. Let's enjoy the security and confidence it brings and the connection we feel within ourselves and with the Divine.

As thought becomes less scary, we don't see it as something we need to control. We can allow our body to feel what we think, to do its thing and to let thoughts pass, and know that we'll be OK. We don't have to fear thought storms. A thought storm is just like a 24-hour bug passing through our system: it will run its course and eventually clear.

We no longer have to be victims of our thinking. The unhealthy intensity of life and the drama of it all seems to fade. We no longer need to fight the waves. We gracefully learn how to ride the wave: the wave of life via thought. We have been talking about what is behind the human experience. It's a very narrow discussion, but very deep. The gift of realizing that the only way we ever have an experience is via thought frees us. We are feeling what we think about life, rather than feeling life itself.

It is simple. There is a spiritual, mystical nature to our experience. It is liberating when we notice it instead of trying to control it. That's when miracles and transformation happen. Our relationship to our thinking, our relationship to other people's behaviors and our relationship to our circumstances all shift when we see where our experience of life really comes from. Life is happening from the inside out. We can't control the waves, but we can learn how to surf. As we learn to ride the wave of our thinking, life becomes not just a bearable ride, but an enjoyable one. May we all be blessed with continuous insight and wisdom to guide us while experiencing life with grace, serenity and happiness more and more. Most of all, may we feel our deep connection to the Divine, and may we let Him guide us on our journey.

MINDWORKS
Health from the Inside Out

For information about seminars, webinars, speaking engagements or counseling, please contact:

Aviva Barnett, LSW
aviva@mwmindworks.com
973.865.9062
mwmindworks.com

Made in the USA
Middletown, DE
01 May 2016